SIR HUMPHREY GILBERT

SIR HUMPHREY GILBERT, PIONEER

Sir Humphrey Gilbert

ELIZABETH'S RACKETEER

By
DONALD BARR CHIDSEY

WILDSIDE PRESS

CONTENTS

I. THE FINE ART OF FAILURE	1
II. RELIGION AND POLITICS	6
III. ELIZABETH WAITS	10
IV. HIS FIRST FIGHT	19
V. AN ARMCHAIR SAILOR	25
VI. SPECTACULAR SHAN O'NEIL	34
VII. THE COUSINS CAUSE TROUBLE	41
VIII. THE QUALITY OF MERCY	48
IX. HOME LIFE, DEBATES, MAGIC	55
X. A THANKLESS JOB	63
XI. EXPERIMENTS IN DECEIT	70
XII. ANOTHER GRAND IDEA	78
XIII. A CELEBRATED ARGUMENT	85
XIV. ALWAYS THE PIONEER	93
XV. FROBISHER AMONG THE ESKIMOS	101
XVI. PIRACY, LTD.	111
XVII. KNOLLYS BACKS OUT	120
XVIII. A HUSHED-UP AFFAIR	127
XIX. "THE MASTER THIEF OF THE UNKNOWN WORLD"	137
XX. DESIGNING ARCADIA	146
XXI. THE GREAT ADVENTURE BEGINS	158
XXII. OVER THE BOUNDING MAIN	165
XXIII. DISASTER	176
XXIV. THE END OF A PIONEER	188
BIBLIOGRAPHY	196
INDEX	199

ILLUSTRATIONS

SIR HUMPHREY GILBERT, PIONEER	*Frontispiece*
	Facing page
TYPICAL FIGHTING-SHIP OF THE TIME	116
SIR HUMPHREY TAKES NEWFOUNDLAND	178
THE GILBERT MAP	*End papers*

SIR HUMPHREY GILBERT

CHAPTER I

THE FINE ART OF FAILURE

IT DOESN'T pay to be a pioneer. The shores of history are strewn with wreckage which represents intelligent, earnest, but unsuccessful efforts to get to some place before anybody else got there, or to do something nobody else ever had done—relics, these, of which the layman would have no present knowledge were it not that modern beach-combers (perhaps rendered desperate by the realization that everything else had been gleaned) have concentrated on these bits of wreckage, and clamoured about them, insisting upon their significance in the scheme of things.

Which is all to the good. With stories of success and grand achievement we have been surfeited. Recipes, formulas, "secrets" of success, have been heaped upon us too liberally. And the fine art of failure has been ignored.

Victory may have its glory; there is poetry in defeat. While success dazzles, stuns by its very brilliancy, failure is of the stuff we all understand; we know it, feel at home with it; it is *gemüdlich*. Moreover, one failure, properly examined, contains far more instruction than any tale of a goal achieved. So if you like lessons, the wreckage is filled with them.

Humphrey Gilbert was a failure. He was an exceptionally intelligent man, energetic, well-born and well-connected, far-sighted, ambitious, likable, inestimably courageous. But he was a born pioneer. All his life he was ruled by a passion for doing something new, sailing seas no man ever had sailed before, establishing an empire in far-away lands nobody ever had seen. It doesn't (be it repeated) pay. Examine the wreckage. Before Fulton, many a hard-working and well-informed scientist invented the steamboat—and got only bankruptcy for his pains. Who remembers the predecessors of the Wright brothers, or cares anything about their bruises and broken bones? And how many laboratory workers, do you suppose, scorched their hands and faces, and endured the derision of their associates, before that mediæval monk discovered gunpowder for the Western World? Even old Admiral Columbus, an exception among exceptions, died in jail while less original seamen were making money along the trail he had blazed.

Contemporaries were fond of referring to "gentle Humphrey Gilbert." It is well not to be misled. The man was anything but "gentle" in the modern sense of that word. He was a dreamer, yes, and a scholar; but he was also a man of action, who on the field of battle could be as brutal, as bloodthirsty, as any personage in history—far more so than most of them.

It is likely that the adjective referred rather to his breeding. In that sense, he *was* "gentle." In an age when two- and three-generation knights and noblemen, whose grandfathers or great-grandfathers had been mere artisans, were beginning to force their way into the pilot-house of the English ship of state, Humphrey Gilbert was emphatically of the old school. Forward-looking in other respects, he was a reactionary in this. He had a lively sense of family, and he never permitted any acquaintances or associates to forget that his ancestors had been landowners in England before the Conquest.

The Gilberts were of Norman origin, very proud and straight, a commendable sort of family. Evidently they coöperated effectively when their countrymen undertook to occupy England; for William, after he had completed his conquering, rewarded them liberally.

They lived in Devon. They had always lived in Devon, since they had ceased living in Normandy, back in the dim ages. It was their world, that county, for many centuries. They were related to all of the important Devonshire families, and they rarely stirred from home except when their sovereign called them to war. Humphrey seems to have been the first of the Gilberts to be bitten by wanderlust. Probably some of his predecessors, certainly some of his cousins, conducted or invested in sundry piratical enterprises from time to time; but none of them ever dreamed of founding empires, crossing oceans, opening up new worlds.

Humphrey's father was Sir Otho Gilbert, a stout country gentleman who was married to his cousin Katherine, daughter of Sir Philip Champernoun, of Modbury, Kent. They had four sons and a daughter. The daughter, Katherine, married George Raleigh, half-brother of the celebrated Sir Walter Raleigh. The sons, in the order of their ages, were John, Humphrey, Adrian, and Otis. John led an uneventful life, remaining in Devonshire and fulfilling his duties as a large landowner. Otis died young. Adrian, like Humphrey, was first a soldier and later a sailor—but at heart a sailor all the time. He became almost as famous as his brother, our present subject.

There is very little to tell about Humphrey's childhood and youth, because there's very little that we know of it for certain. We are not even sure of the date of his birth; probably it was 1539.

Sir Otho had estates at Greenway, on the River Dart, and at Compton, near Torbay; and manors at Brixham, Sandridge, Hansford, Galmeton, etc. Probably he lived most of the time at Greenway. It was a comfortable, homely sort of place. The river, at this point, looks more like a lake, a sleepy sort of lake, which reflects an amiable, sleepy sort of countryside.

Compton Castle would have been a more romantic background for such a person as Humphrey Gilbert; but it is likely that Sir Otho preferred comfort to romance, and Compton Castle assuredly was not very comfortable. It *was* mediæval, though, and with a vengeance. It had no moat; but it had a postern gate with a portcullis, and many machicolated bartizans, four grim towers, a wall twenty feet high, a secret underground passage, and of course its full allotment of ghosts.

Humphrey Gilbert used to sign himself, in later life, "of Compton." But Sir Otho preferred Greenway.

They were well-to-do, but not rich. They were important persons in their own county, and not without influence at Court; but in the world of big affairs, in London town, they were not esteemed great.

Humphrey was a mere lad when his father died. The will, probated June 16, 1547, left Greenway and Compton to the oldest son, John. Humphrey inherited Hansford and some lands and tenements in Borington and Offewell. John continued to live at Greenway, an earnest and unimaginative young lord of land, while Humphrey and Adrian went to live with their uncle, Philip Penkewell, and baby Otis remained with his mother. *She* remarried—with the disconcerting promptitude characteristic of widows in those days—her second husband being Walter Raleigh, an obscure but proud cousin, to whom she bore, among other offspring, a boy who was named Walter, Junior, and who in later years was knighted by an adoring queen.

Thus Humphrey Gilbert and Walter Raleigh were half-brothers, sons of the same mother, though there was a difference of fourteen years in their ages. They were also fast friends. Each supported the other in everything that he did or tried to do. Each defended the other against his enemies. They believed in one another loved one another, helped one another. They were an extraordinary pair of men. It would be interesting to know more about their mother.

CHAPTER II

RELIGION AND POLITICS

THE same year Otho Gilbert died there was another death of much greater consequence to England and to the world in general. The much-married Henry VIII expired, leaving the kingdom to his puny son, Edward.

It was a time of vast political excitement. Nobody knew just what was going to happen next; and poor little Edward was hardly a reassuring sort of monarch. In fact, Edward did not rule at all. Somerset ruled for him, as Protector, and later Warwick ruled, with no particular title. Both were makeshifts.

Technically, England was a Protestant nation then, having but recently severed relations with the Vatican; but nobody but a fool would venture to predict what she would be a year hence, or even a few months hence. Edward was a Protestant. The Gilberts and their various cousins were all pronounced Protestants. But Henry's oldest child, Mary, who probably would succeed Edward, was a sincere Catholic, and north of the Humber and west of the Severn, England still was Catholic and feudal.

Edward came down with both smallpox and measles in April, 1552, and he died a year later, at Greenwich, fifteen years, eight months and three weeks old.

At that time, the only other offspring of the dead Henry VIII, Mary and Elizabeth, were both legally bastards. It was all very confusing.

Mary, the ardent Catholic, had the best claim, and she got the throne; but she got a welter of trouble with it. There was Elizabeth, and there was another female claimant, poor Lady Jane Gray. Some conniving person had changed the wording of Edward's will, making "Lady Jane's heirs male" into "Lady Jane *and her* heirs male," and this inspired a multitude of plots which culminated in some noisy bloodletting, a general rush of over-enthusiastic Protestants to the Continent, and the removal of the pretty pawn's head.

As for Elizabeth, she was at that time a very quiet, very careful, and studious young woman. A Protestant, on paper, she was willing enough to attend mass in order to keep up appearances, and to mark time and avert suspicion by asking for instruction in the mysteries of the Holy Roman Church. Elizabeth was in a dangerous position, and she knew it; and admirably she kept her mouth shut, her ears stopped, her eyes closed.

Then Mary complicated matters still further, and added to her own unpopularity, by marrying Philip, son of the Emperor Charles V. Philip, the hope of the Catholic world, was a thin, nervous, slow-thinking man. He was, then, Prince Regent of Spain and of Sicily, and he was also Archduke of Milan, Archduke of Burgundy, Archduke of Brabant, Count of Hapsburg, Count of Flanders, Count of Tyrol. . . . His father considered even this insufficient, now that Philip was to marry a reigning queen, so he created his favourite son King of Naples and of Jerusalem, a brand-new title invented for the occasion.

Philip had a stern sense of duty, and always did what he thought he should do as a Hapsburg. His duty in this case was twofold: he was to bring England back into the Holy Roman Church, and he was to get England into a war with the Emperor's old enemy, France.

So he arrived, on July 23, 1554, resplendent in white kid covered with gold embroidery, and with a French-grey satin surcoat. England was anything but enthusiastic. The government, at Edward's death, had been £200,000 in debt—a staggering sum then—and paying the Fuggers and Schetz interest at the rate of 14 per cent. Wars are always expensive, and quite obviously this newly arrived consort had his heart set on promoting a war. Not that Philip was a belligerent sort of person, naturally. He was quite the opposite, hating battle and all the noisiness of military display. But his father needed England's assistance in the more or less perpetual conflict between the Hapsburgs and the house of Valois, and so Philip, that obedient, conscientious son, set about causing a war—and eventually succeeded, though it was a half-hearted sort of war at best, as far as England was concerned, and it didn't last long.

What Humphrey Gilbert was doing all this time we do not know. He went to Eton and to Oxford, though probably he did not remain long at either place. It was the custom to shove students through the universities rather rapidly then, and to start them very young. It was not at all unusual for a boy to be an Oxford graduate, as Gilbert apparently was, at the age of fourteen or fifteen.[1]

When he was at home, Humphrey Gilbert must have witnessed many scenes of religious excitement and listened to much talk about the political and religious opinions and activities of the new monarch. In that part of England, the peasantry generally was Catholic in sympathy, but the upper classes and the seafaring men or men interested in commerce by sea, were generally Protestant. The Gilberts and all their cousins were bitterly opposed to the proposed marriage of Mary to the Emperor's son. Gilbert's mother is reported to have spent considerable time comforting persons jailed for their anti-Roman beliefs and utterances. And his step-

[1] It was at about this time that a regulation was enacted at Oxford prohibiting the students from playing marbles!

father, Walter Raleigh, Sr., got himself into trouble one day when he tried to persuade a peasant woman to throw away her beads. The woman raised the countryside, creating a mob, and Walter Raleigh was imprisoned in a church steeple and was very lucky to escape with his life.

The boy's cousins, Sir Arthur Champernoun and Sir Peter Carew, a couple of gentlemen thugs, were in charge of raising rebellion in Devonshire, in the middle of March, 1554, while Courtenay did the same thing in Cornwall, Sir James Crofts did it in Herefordshire, Sir Hugh Wyatt, the general leader of the concerted uprising, was busy in Kent, and other reformed persons were similarly engaged in other parts of the kingdom. Courtenay babbled, and the plot was exploded prematurely by desperate men. It was a terrible failure. Champernoun was arrested, but subsequently released. The Council, in London, sent for Sir Peter Carew, who had been on his way from the capital to his home county. He heard that they were seeking him, realized that the game was up, and persuaded Walter Raleigh to take him across the Channel. Walter Raleigh had his own bark. Peter Carew had several ships, and he used them, with a French base, for mauling Spanish commerce in those parts, until, years later, he was admitted back into England.

All these men were close relatives of Humphrey Gilbert, persons among whom he had been raised. It is impossible to believe that he himself was not vastly excited by this agitation.

But he must have become even more excited when they placed him into the very centre of the swirl of plots and counter-plots, by getting him a position in the household of the Princess Elizabeth.

CHAPTER III

ELIZABETH WAITS

WE THINK of Elizabeth, usually, as a tall, thin, hooked-nosed female in a red wig—a woman with blackening teeth, glittering eyes, a weak stomach, and a sharp tongue. We think of her garbed in stiff, ornate costumes, a person who swore in four languages at foreign ambassadors, frowning, ranting, dazzling; or, in another mood, as thumping her favourites on the back, tweeking their ears, roaring with laughter as she exchanged dirty stories with them.

The picture is accurate enough—except for the height; she was not tall, though most of her portraits make her look tall. It is, at least, as accurate as anything pertaining to Elizabeth ever can be. But it is a picture of the queen, not of the princess whom Humphrey Gilbert first met; it is a picture of a woman seated firmly upon a firm throne, not of the girl who was never certain whether she would sleep that night in a cell or in a palace, a girl by law a bastard but by accident of birth also the potential heroine of an army of religious fanatics and political tricksters, a girl who might expect at any time to have her head either crowned or removed.

Elizabeth was a little over twenty years old when Humphrey Gilbert entered her service, presumably as a page. He was fifteen or sixteen, intensely loyal, scholarly, adoring. He found her a mild-mannered, very quiet young woman, cautious, soft-spoken, wise beyond her years, but possessed of a convenient appearance of innocence. Had she been anything else, she probably would have achieved the axe rather than the crown. For she was, and for some years had been—and for some years yet was to continue to be—in a very dangerous position. And likewise those who attended her never were sure of their own positions or the firmness of their hold upon life.

But the very charm of sixteenth-century politics, the reason for its fascination, was just this element of hourly danger. The men seemed truly to love risk in those days. Youthfully, they were thrilled. They walked with the lightnings playing all about them, and they sang as they walked, glorying in this uncertainty, delighted by the ever-nearness of violent death.

It was Aunt Katherine, in all probability, who got Humphrey the position in the Princess's household. Aunt Katherine was by birth a Champernoun, and she had been married to William Ashley, who was a near relation of Anne Boleyn, Elizabeth's mother. Now it is a curious thing about Elizabeth, that while she never mentioned her mother's name, publicly or privately, if such mention could possibly be avoided, she was uniformly kind to her mother's numerous relatives. For Kat Ashley—she always called her Kat—she seems to have had a warm personal devotion. Mrs. Ashley had been appointed governess of the Princess even before the death of Henry VIII, and she continued in this capacity all her long life. Elizabeth, to be sure, had more sound knowledge in her small head at the age of fifteen than Kat Ashley possessed all her life. But the woman was beloved as a confidante and a friend; and for all her exasperating fondness for match-making, and for all her talent for getting herself and her mistress into trouble, Elizabeth clung to her faithfully.

Certainly some strong influence was necessary to get the appointment. For Elizabeth was a very popular young woman, legally a nobody, but potentially the next queen of England, at once the pawn of discontented statesmen all over the kingdom and the hope of Protestants all over Europe. The Venetian Resident at London, Michiele, recorded the fact that "every lord in the Kingdom is seeking to enter her service himself, or place one of his sons or brothers in it, such being the love and affection borne her."

It may be that ambition, the thrill of a big gamble, the love of danger, also had something to do with this rush of applications.

Wyatt's rebellion had been timed to start when Philip of Spain landed in England to claim his bride, the Queen; but it was bungled, and before that event the official torturers and executioners were busy with such plotters as had not previously made good their escape. Wyatt himself, screaming in pain on the rack, confessed what the questioners desired him to confess—that Elizabeth had been a party to the treason. Later, just before they chopped off his head, he retracted this confession: it had been wrung out of him by torture, he said, and it wasn't true.

But they sent for Elizabeth. She took five days to travel thirty-three miles, complaining that ill-health caused the delay—which might or might not have been the truth. Queen Mary refused to see her, and she was thrown into London Tower. But she steadfastly pleaded her innocence and they were unable to prove anything against her, so two months later she was released. She went back to Woodstock, and her followers exhaled with relief, for another crisis had been passed.

It was shortly after this that Humphrey Gilbert joined Elizabeth's household. She liked him. He was quiet, loyal, scholarly. The Princess, too wary to take any active part in politics, was devoting herself to learning, and Humphrey Gilbert made excellent intellectual companionship. How he himself had managed to learn so much in so short a period of study is not clear; but we know that he was familiar with Latin, Greek, French, and Spanish, and with poetry and philosophy and theology; and in addition, he had ideas on more practical subjects. He had a lively, eager, inquiring mind —just the sort of man Elizabeth liked. They used to read together, and talk, by the hour.

Learned men argue still, probably always will argue, the question of just how Roman Catholic England was at this time of change. They never will come to any satisfactory decision about this. Certainly a good part of the peasantry, particularly in the north and west, were papal in sympathy; but except in the north, the aristocracy was inclined to favor the Reformation, and the merchants and seamen were almost unanimously Protestant. It has been pointed out that there is perhaps some connection between the Protestantism of the powerful trade classes and the fact that most of England's outside business was conducted with the reformed peoples of the Low Countries, while practically all the English pirates depended upon the ships of ultra-Catholic Spain and Portugal for their pickings. But this is beside the point, which is that the peasantry, however inclined, had very little to say about the matter, and the aristocracy and the merchants, who ran England, were generally opposed to the Pope at Rome, for whatever reasons.

With the ascension of Mary to the throne, England had nominally returned to the fold. But only nominally. As Pollard puts it, "there had been no real reconversion to Rome, and the reconciliation was merely a marriage of convenience." Mass was celebrated openly in the land, and sundry Anglican bishops were burned here and there, creating much hard feeling against the coming of Catholic Philip. It is significant that, whatever the official religion officially was, Parliament solemnly decided that the only appeal the Holy Roman Church could make to the owners of rich abbey lands Henry VIII had confiscated, was to their consciences—and there is no record of such an appeal having met with success.

But careful Elizabeth knew which way the wind was blowing; she understood the intense religious feeling that stimulated her half sister, the Queen, and cannily she trimmed her sails. She went to mass. She listened while priests explained for her edification the mysteries of the Holy Roman Church. She was not formally converted: she managed to stop just short of that. But she was obliging as to outward show, and loud with promises. Whatever mental reservations she may have made were her own business; and historians, prompted by a passion for investigating dead persons' mental affairs, have been able to extract nothing but guesses here.

Elizabeth had enemies—bitter enemies. Indeed, Bishop Gardiner, who hated her with a grand, ecclesiastical hatred, once went so far as to sign a warrant for her execution, when the Queen was ill and Elizabeth was in the Tower; and it was only because the governor of the Tower refused to execute such an order unsigned by the Queen that the Princess retained her life.

But she was clever and brave. She could face her enemies. It was only her friends she had to fear. For altogether too many of those friends she represented salvation, freedom, defeat of the Antichrist; she was the Protestant Champion, even while she attended mass and listened to the teachings of priests; she was the Hope of the World. Indefatigibly they schemed to have her placed upon the throne. She was cognizant of some of these schemes, possibly of all of them; but she was shrewd enough to keep herself technically clear, so that when she protested innocence before a suspicious, fanatical half sister, she sounded convincing—at least, nobody could prove enough against her to call in the headsman.

For to call in the headsman, here, would require a vast amount of proof, indisputable proof. Henry VIII had managed the removal of this young woman's mother without any great legal difficulty; but things were different now. In the first place, the Queen, for all the fact that she has gone down in history unenviably as "Bloody Mary," was a kind-hearted, well-meaning thing, and she bore no grudge against her half sister. And Philip, despised as he was, and still is, by Englishmen, was a careful person, well aware of his own unpopularity on the island, disinclined by nature to any extreme or violent courses, and hopeful always of winning the Princess Elizabeth back into the fold by peaceful means. So that, for all the seeming danger of her position, Elizabeth would have been safe enough if only her friends would let her alone—if only they would wait, as she was willing to wait.

But they were impatient. The Wyatt affair tightened the atmosphere, and for a long time afterward men talked in whispers. "Treason" was the most terrible of all things, then; and almost anything was treason when the Queen and her consort were angry and frightened. About the time Humphrey Gilbert attached himself to the household of the Princess, Parliament passed a bill making it treason even to "pray or desire" that God shorten the Queen's days. No doubt that law was broken many times; but it is significant, none the less. And treason, remember, was inevitably punished by death—not a prompt death, either.

The king of France wrote to Elizabeth, offering her any assistance she might desire, offering her asylum in his kingdom. The king of France, to be sure, was a Catholic; but he was also a Valois, and so an hereditary enemy of Queen Mary's husband. He couldn't have done anything sillier. The letter, of course, was intercepted, and poor Elizabeth was forced to do some further explaining. Calmly, quietly, always with perfect control of her emotions, she talked her way out of this difficulty, persuading the government to believe what was probably the truth—that she had known nothing about this offer, had never invited it or suggested it, and wanted nothing to do with it.

The Spanish ambassador visited her. She was polite, reserved, noncommittal. The French ambassador visited her; she had not changed.

She was moved from Woodstock to Hatfield. She made no objection, obeying meekly.

For some time after her release from the Tower she was allowed practically no attendants. Her large household—poor Elizabeth didn't want it!—annoyed and alarmed the Queen. Then the attendants all were sent away, and the Princess was alone again, and Humphrey Gilbert had nobody upon whom to wait. Still, she was complacent. All she desired, she said, was to be permitted to study; she was a truly remarkable student.

She was ordered to appear before Mary at Hampton Court. She went, practically unattended. But all the gentlemen and yeomen of her household, about sixty in number, forbidden to speak to her or to approach her, lined the road as she travelled and cheered her loudly with adoring looks. It was a touching scene.

If Mary bore Philip a son, or even a daughter, then all Elizabeth's hopes would be extinguished—assuming that she had hopes, which she denied. And for some time it looked as though Mary were going to fulfil her one real function as a royal female. The marriage had been in July, 1554. By November there was an official announcement that Mary was pregnant, and a tremendous flutter this caused! Protestants sighed in despair, muttering that the ways of God are inscrutable. Catholics, cheering, got drunk, and exalted that God's truth always triumphs in the end.

This excitement continued for almost a year—until August, 1555. At any hour, apparently, the child might appear. Official letters announcing the birth were drawn up and addressed to foreign princes, with only the date and the sex to be filled in. Exuberantly, new titles for the child-to-come were devised. Envoys were appointed to bear the glad tidings to continental courts, and were instructed to hold themselves in readiness. There were processions and prayers and special masses and all the rest of it.

But that child never did appear and eventually all hope was abandoned. The Catholics sighed, muttering that the ways of God are inscrutable, while the Protestants, cheering, got drunk, exalting that God's truth always triumphs in the end.

All this enormously increased the importance of the Princess Elizabeth, who only wanted to be left alone so that she could study. Philip began to take a close personal interest in her. Philip had never for an instant lost sight of his mission in England. Apparently he and Mary weren't going to be able to produce a baby, and the next best thing, obviously, was to get for the Princess Elizabeth some good Catholic husband—some one who would keep her well inclined toward the emperor and the Vatican, some reliable, Hapsburg-endorsed prince who was good-natured, not scandalously vicious, and willing to listen to orders. Philip began to make suggestions.

But here Elizabeth was on firm ground. Much as she knew about protesting innocence of treasonous plots, she knew even more about getting rid of unwelcome suitors without giving offence. She had been doing just that as long as she could remember. There had always been somebody who was eager to marry her; there always would be somebody.

Elizabeth listened respectfully to all suggestions, apparently gave deep and long consideration to each, and in the end invariably found some unanswerable objection, hastily protesting, however, that she had no will of her own in the matter and was prepared to be guided by the wishes of her dear half sister and the prince consort.

Say what you will about her, the woman had a genius —not merely a talent, a *genius*—for politics. The way in which she could evade an issue was nothing short of masterly. Not merely for months, but for years, she could find excuses for not making a definite answer to a definite question. Indeed, not merely for years—forever! Though she was a public character from the beginning, though throughout her life she was always between at least two fires, we do not know even today what she really thought about many of the problems which faced her during all her reign and even before her reign. She hesitated magnificently. She still has the whole world guessing.

And in time her waiting game was successful. Philip was called away to tend to Spanish matters, and he never returned to England. Queen Mary wrote to her, asserting that she had no objection to the ascension of Elizabeth in the event of her own death, and begging her to pay the throne's staggering bills and to keep the true religion intact. What Mary meant by the true religion was perfectly clear. What Elizabeth meant, nobody ever has been able to learn.

And then, very quietly, poor Mary died, and Elizabeth became queen of England and of Ireland.

CHAPTER IV

HIS FIRST FIGHT

TO HUMPHREY GILBERT, serving the Queen was both a duty and a delight. He was wholeheartedly a courtier—not a climbing statesman, not a parliamentarian, certainly not a ranting reformer, but an old-fashioned, knee-bending, flattery-murmuring courtier. What the Queen said was right, and it was the only thing that *was* right.

He had high ideals about chivalry, too, and it may be that these played a part in his devoted adherence to his monarch. After all, she was a woman, and at this time she was a young and not unattractive woman. He had been with her during much of that troublesome period when she was in daily danger of trial and death, when plots were exploding around her like firecrackers, and only the coolest kind of conduct, the shrewdest sort of manœuvring, had kept her head upon her shoulders. And even now she was seated on a throne that was none too firmly placed. Even though she was some five years older than Humphrey Gilbert, it is likely that he felt a protective impulse heightening his adoration. All her earlier courtiers felt that way about Elizabeth.

Still faced with stunning difficulties, the woman handled herself superbly. Mary died on November 17, 1558,[1] and on the following day Elizabeth was pro-

---

[1] This is according to the so-called Old Time. The Gregorian Calender, which was established in most continental nations in 1582, was not officially adopted in England until the eighteenth century—perhaps because a Catholic plot was suspected. But even 1582 was only one year

claimed Queen of England, France, and Ireland, "Defender of the Faith, etc." That "etc." replaced the customary words, "Supreme Head of the Church." For nobody was quite certain, yet, what the state religion was. Elizabeth's first official act was the issuance of a proclamation forbidding "the breach, alteration, or changes of any order or usage presently established." England, at any rate, was not going Protestant again in one jump. Nothing must be done too hastily.

Philip of Spain was not in England at this time. He had been gone for more than a year, having achieved his Anglo-French war and finding many things to busy him on the Continent. To Elizabeth, upon her ascension, he extended the expected congratulations, and then promptly began again to suggest suitable husbands for her. He proposed his own son, Don Carlos—a youth utterly mad, utterly vicious, who was subsequently assassinated, very quietly, by the orders of his own father. He proposed Emmanuel Philibert of Savoy, an amiable princeling who was under the Hapsburg thumb. And finally he proposed himself. All three of these suggestions Elizabeth put aside with all possible courtesy and after much delay in each case. She was not looking for a husband, thank you.

She settled down to the task of restoring the national credit. England was pitifully poor. The royal expenditures at the time of Henry VIII's death had been about £56,000 a year. Edward left a debt of £200,000. Mary left a debt of nearly £250,000: she had exceeded her revenues by more than 40 per cent during much of her reign. The royal expenditures for the last fiscal half-year of Mary's reign were £267,000. During the first fiscal half-year of Elizabeth's reign they were only £108,000. Within six months of the beginning of her

before the death of Humphrey Gilbert. Consequently, every date in this book will be according to the Old Time.

rule Elizabeth was able to borrow money in Antwerp at only 10 per cent, as compared with the 14 per cent both Edward and Mary had been obliged to pay. The world might have some doubt about this new Queen's religious ideas, if any, but it could not question her thriftiness.

However, with this, as with other knotty problems with which Elizabeth was obliged to cope during the early years of her reign, Humphrey Gilbert had little or nothing to do. He was no statesman and no business man. It was said of him that at Oxford he had been proficient in all his studies, but had been particularly diligent in the study of navigation and the art of warfare. Geography, a little-known branch of learning— a vague and romantic study which compared with alchemy, astrology, and magic—fascinated the young man. He was fumbling with books about sea currents and wind tendencies of the Western Hemisphere, with maps and charts and sea cards; and he was interviewing sailors, navigators, merchants, adventurers. He was beginning to dream that great dream of his which eventually was to send hundreds of men to watery graves and to start England on a career of empire-building.

At the same time he desired to be a man of action. He lacked the capital to launch his own grandiose scheme of exploration and colonization, and his older brother, John, who had inherited the bulk of Sir Otho's modest fortune, was not interested. So Humphrey Gilbert looked about for a convenient war, there being nothing else to do. He came from a fighting family, and he might as well learn that business.

The war Philip had managed to stir up between England and France, though technically still in existence when Elizabeth mounted the throne, died a quiet and unremarkable death very soon after that event. But this did not mean that a little informal battling could not be found for adventurous younger sons like the Gilbert scion. He was dispatched to help in the defence of Havre de Grace.[2]

In the course of long-drawn-out marriage negotiations she was to conduct with various foreign, and Catholic, princes, Queen Elizabeth was wont to remind the representatives of parents of those princes that it would be most inadvisable for a monarch to tolerate the open practice of two conflicting religions in the same kingdom. She was all for uniformity of worship, in England. Elsewhere, however, it was different. France, for instance.

In France there had begun that long series of civil wars with the Huguenots on one side, the Catholic and pro-Spanish Guises on the other, and the Catholic but moderate Montmorencys somewhere in between—for wars were more or less family matters then. The Huguenots were not numerous, but they were determined, and they were well led by the Bourbons, representatives of the third great house of France. Now the Huguenots held some Channel ports, around which most of the fighting was concerned. The powerful Guise forces, with the backing of the French crown, had cooped them up in Rouen, Dieppe, and Havre de Grace, and all three cities were in serious danger. The Huguenots appealed to Elizabeth as a Protestant, and when that appeared to have no effect, they appealed to her as a business woman.

She struck a hard bargain. For sweet religion's sake she would help them in their defence of the Channel cities, to the extent of 100,000 crowns and 6,000 soldiers, provided that she was guaranteed possession of Havre de Grace until the much-lamented Calais, last

[2] Almost all English histories refer to this seaport as New Haven. Today it is known simply as Havre.

of the English holdings in France, which had fallen shortly before Mary's death, had been restored to England. To these terms the desperate Huguenots agreed.

To be sure, Elizabeth was not at war with France. This, however, made no difference. Of formal warfare she had a lively horror: it was dangerous, it was uncertain, and it was expensive. But unofficial war could be given another name and could be made very useful, and cheap. Elizabeth sent the men to France, and one of them was Humphrey Gilbert.

The Huguenots objected that she was sending them too few men—that she was giving them enough to hold their cities, perhaps, but not enough to win their war. But that, as it happened, was precisely what she desired.

But, the Huguenots then protested, unless she sent them further help they would not even be able to hold their cities and the Protestant cause would be crushed in France and the English would be driven out; Elizabeth would not get Calais back, after all. She did not believe them. But they were correct. The Guises stormed and captured Dieppe and Rouen, and that particular civil war was ended. The English forces, all established at Havre de Grace, were so notified, and the suggestion was made that they get back to the island where they belonged.

Now the English forces had been forbidden to take the field. Elizabeth had promised to supply them for defensive purposes only, and she was not prepared to go any further than the terms of her bargain. But they *had* been ordered to hold Havre de Grace, and when their commander, Dudley, Earl of Warwick, was told by the French that the war was over and he might as well go back home and take all his men with him, he stoutly refused to obey. His queen had told him to hold Havre de Grace, and he was going to hold Havre de Grace. He was not taking orders from any Frenchman.

He redoubled his preparation for defence of the city. If they wanted him to get out, let them come and *put* him out!

The French in Havre de Grace themselves didn't fancy the presence of Englishmen there. The townspeople, or some of them, were plotting to turn the city over to their fellow countrymen, the besiegers. So the townspeople were turned out of Havre de Grace, every one of them, and the English made ready to repel boarders.

The French made repeated attempts to recapture the city and there was some spirited fighting, in which Humphrey Gilbert blooded his maiden sword, and in the course of which, on June 5, 1563, he was wounded.

The French were repelled; but a more puissant enemy was at work inside the city walls. The plague appeared. English soldiers were dying by the dozens, by the hundreds. Reinforcements were dispatched, but they could not arrive fast enough to fill the places made vacant in the ranks by this unseen foe. Nobody seemed to know just what to do about the plague, which was new to Englishmen. Nobody seemed to know just what it was. But it was killing soldiers faster than fellow soldiers could bury them; and at last, on July 28th, Warwick surrendered the city. He obtained honorable terms and retired with banners flying. His men brought the plague back to England, where it killed, in time, hundreds of thousands of persons. Humphrey Gilbert, so far as we can learn, never was attacked by it.

He was a soldier now. He had served "with great commendation." But there were no further wars handy, formal or otherwise, so he returned to his library and to his dreams—he had become a scholar again.

CHAPTER V

AN ARMCHAIR SAILOR

ETON and Oxford had not completed his education; they had only launched it. His mind was amazingly active. However crowded the events of his life, he always found time for the study of some new subject.

He was a friend of poets, and, being an Elizabethan courtier, no mean poetaster himself. He was familiar with the classics. He had strong ideas on the current educational system, and in this he was a reformer. The long, eager, intellectual conversations with Elizabeth were not so frequent, now that she was queen and had little leisure for such things. But she had liked those conversations as much as he; and she still could put aside matters of state, occasionally, and revert to princess days in his company. "Her Majesty had a special good liking for him," old Hooker records, "and very oftentimes would familiarly discourse and confer with him in matters of learning."

But Elizabeth, though she possessed a keen mind, was no dreamer, but a highly practical woman; she was interested in the here and the now, and in these alone; and she never troubled herself about the other side of the world, or what might happen one hundred years hence or even one year hence. And so it was that she did not condescend to talk with Humphrey Gilbert on his one grand passion; she had no patience with and no time for hearing the details of his life's ambition.

The wonder is not that this man was interested in matters nautical. The wonder is rather that he had not taken to the sea as a boy, instead of spending so much time on land. His heart was on the sea from the beginning. His West Country cousins were all seafaring men, or men heavily interested in seafaring ventures. He was related to virtually all the great English sea families of the time—the Gorges, Fortescues, Champernouns, Grenvilles, Raleighs, Drakes. He deeply and actively sympathized with the Huguenots—his cousin, Gawen Champernoun, had been married to Gabrielle, daughter of the great Huguenot leader, the Count de Montgomerie, and Humphrey Gilbert himself had fought side by side with Huguenots at Havre de Grace—and the Huguenots comprised most of the great French sea families. The Gilberts came of pure Norman stock, and were not the Normans celebrated sailors?

In the beginning, he was an armchair sailor. The phrase sounds derogatory but it is not meant to be that. The truth is there were all too few of these armchair sailors in England at that time. Seventy-five years after Columbus's first transatlantic voyage, English ignorance of geography was astounding. It was known that the world was round, and something about latitude and longitude also was known, though not much. But geography, when it was taught at all in English universities, was hopelessly classical—it was Mela and Pliny, Strabo and Ptolemy, nothing since. The world still was divided into three parts instead of four; and there was scarcely anything to indicate, in libraries and in studies and classrooms, that two vast continents had been discovered on the other side of the Atlantic, and that the oblique spheroid upon which we live was many times larger than had previously been supposed and quite different in shape and general make-up.

Enormous, virtually illimitable fields of endeavour for that most exciting of all pastimes—the acquisition of knowledge—had been opened up by Christopher Columbus. Scholars and men of action were challenged in a voice equally commanding to both. The Spaniards and the Portuguese were prompt to answer that challenge; they were cruising here, there, and elsewhere, penetrating this wilderness, surmounting those mountains, overtoppling whole empires, rebuilding new worlds—and, incidentally, making millions. The French, at first, were too busy with their civil wars to do more than tinker with the subject at odd intervals, and the English seemed perfectly content with their own tight little island, and not at all eager to learn about the other side of the globe.

Against this complacency a small, keen, courageous group of men was fighting. And not the least of these, perhaps the greatest of them, was Humphrey Gilbert.

Yes, he was an armchair sailor. He read every book and manuscript available on the subject, though these were pitifully few. From the tireless Richard Hakluyt, a humble but invaluable member of this group, he learned about the voyages of the Cabots; of Armagil Waad, the "English Columbus" who sailed to Cape Breton; of Willoughby, who lost his life trying to find a north-eastern passage, around Russia, to Cathay; of Chancellor, who lost *his* life searching for Willoughby; of John Locke, who went to Guinea, and William Towerson, who went there a little later, twice; of Robert Tomson and his extraordinary (if true) Mexican experience; of Stephen Borough, who discovered the entrance to the Kara Sea and explored the coast of Nova Zembla; of William Hawkins and Robert Reniger, who made earlier voyages to Guinea and to Brazil; of Anthony Jenkinson, who went to Archangel, up the Dwina to Moscow, down the Volga, across the Caspian Sea, and as far as Bokhara. Some of these men Humphrey Gilbert knew personally—Hawkins and Jenkinson certainly, and probably some of the others. They were all Englishmen, and their accounts of their voyages were available to fellow Englishmen.

But all this was a mere fluttering of butterflies compared with the work the Spaniards and Portuguese had accomplished. And the Spaniards and Portuguese were jealously guarding their data concerning routes to the far corners of the world. Their pilots were not allowed to take employment with other nations. Their colonies were permitted to trade only with the mother country. The narratives of their seamen were kept under lock and key, and were state secrets, translation being forbidden. They wanted the New World to themselves. A Pope, Alexander VI, *née* Rodriguez Borgia, had given it to them, and they meant to keep it.

Nevertheless, state secrets, even in those days, had a trick of getting out of strong boxes and hopping international boundaries. In spite of all the efforts of the Peninsular nations to keep these works to themselves, the writings of Peter Martyr, Oviedo, Domara, Maffaei, Perreira and others were beginning to appear in French or English translations, or both. Sebastian Muenster's valuable *Cosmography* was published in English. The works of Mercator were studied. And the *Cosmographical Glasse*, the first English book of geography—though it is remarkable for no other reason—was written in 1559 by a Cambridge physician, William Cunningham.

Humphrey Gilbert was absorbed in these things. He was intensely interested in navigation, and impatient with the uneducated English sea captains who did not keep good records of their long voyages. Like the other armchair sailors of Elizabeth's time, he seized eagerly upon records of foreign mariners; for the English scholars were trying to learn what the English men of action couldn't or wouldn't tell them.

Richard Eden was such an one. It was he who trans-

AN ARMCHAIR SAILOR

lated into English, and published, Pigabetta's narrative of Magellan's *Discovery*, and who wrote and published the *Decades of the New World* and *A Treatise of the New India*—musty museum pieces today, but in those times vastly illuminating volumes of knowledge not elsewhere available. Richard Eden was secretary to the Vidame Chartres, commander of the Huguenot forces at the siege of Havre de Grace, and it is impossible to suppose that the youthful Captain Humphrey Gilbert did not seek him out there many times for consultation on what was the life passion of each.

The scholar-soldier also met at about this time, probably at Havre de Grace, the renowned French geographer, Andrew Thevitt.

It was from Havre de Grace, too, that Villegagnon and Jean Ribault had sailed with groups of Huguenots for the New World wilderness and unmolested worship. Both of these colonization expeditions—almost a full century earlier than the first Puritan movement to New England—met with disaster. But when Humphrey Gilbert was in Havre de Grace, then the greatest Huguenot seaport, there must have been much talk about them; and no doubt he had a further opportunity to increase his knowledge of America.

Soon after his return to England he became a member of the Merchant Adventurers, a company of men interested in discovering and developing new trade routes for English ships. Sebastian Cabot—swaggering, boasting, a colossal liar, probably a traitor as well, but indisputably one of the greatest mariners of all time—was governor of the Merchant Adventurers. Humphrey Gilbert, though one of the least wealthy, was one of the most active and most valuable members of this company. He invented a spherical instrument with a compass of variation for the perfect proving of longitude: he complained persistently that English sea captains on northern voyages made no allowance for the fact that the lines of longitude drew closer together the further north they went, but proceeded always as though they were sailing the earth exactly at the equator.

He also wrote careful directions for the pricking of sea cards—the sixteenth century equivalent of ships' logs—with certain rules for determining on its first discovery how far a bay or a strait stretched inland.

Whether this work was of any real immediate value to the art of navigation we have no way of determining today. But it does argue years of study and work on the part of Humphrey Gilbert.

Most of his fellow enthusiasts of the Merchant Adventurers believed that the best route to Asia and Asia's uncountable riches, for Englishmen, was north-east, around Russia. Humphrey Gilbert did not agree. He believed in the existence of a practicable north-west passage. He believed in this with all his heart and soul—with a passionate sincerity it is difficult to understand in this cool, skeptical twentieth century. But for the time he was overruled, and the north-east passage occupied the attention and commanded the capital of most of such men as were eager to expand England and England's commerce.

These men, remember, were not numerous. There is a popular impression, I think, that in the so-called "spacious" days of Queen Elizabeth, England generally was surcharged with excitement about the New World; that England then was overpopulated, straining, ready to smear itself over half the habitable globe; that merchants were prepared to risk their fortunes, scholars their time, and sailors their lives, in order to open up new seas, new lands.

Nothing could be further from the truth. So far from being overpopulated, England needed all her men at home—or so it was supposed—and emigration was strictly forbidden, even private gentlemen who desired to travel or to study on the Continent being obliged to get special permission to leave the country. England was poor. Spanish gold, pouring into Europe from the newly opened mines of the Americas, had dealt a sudden, terrific blow to the value of her currency. She did not have much money to invest in any but the very safest enterprises. Only a small group of students was in the least concerned with the new geography; the majority of teachers, writers, and professors obstinately considered geography a closed subject, and clung to their beloved Greeks. As for the seamen, they might be soever courageous, but the Peninsular nations left them very little of the New World to explore. Mexico, Florida, all the West Indies, Central America, South America—these belonged to Spain, and jealously Spain guarded them. The Canaries, the Azores, practically all of central and southern Africa, and what parts of Brazil Spain didn't own, belonged to Portugal; and Portugal had no intention of permitting English ships to trade there. Except for lone adventurers, who were for the most part pirates, English seamen had to content themselves with the lucrative but inglorious trade with the Low Countries, which then constituted more than 80 per cent of England's commerce, or with fishing off Ireland, possibly sometimes off Iceland, Greenland, or even the Grand Banks.

Nor was there any official encouragement for the farsighted men who desired to push into remoter parts of the world. Elizabeth had no desire to hear of English ships battered to bits on unnamed coasts, English seamen drowned in waters thousands of miles away. Trade, in its immediate sense, she could understand and appreciate. Pounds and shillings recorded in ink, in ledgers one could read, were clear enough to her. She wanted money but she was never a gambler. And without her permission, whether formal or informal, it was impossible to be a first-class pirate, much less an empire-builder.

If Humphrey Gilbert had possessed the money, and if Elizabeth had consented, he would have gone cruising in search of a north-west passage much earlier than he did. But he was a younger son with an income barely sufficient for his own personal needs. His brother John was a phlegmatic country gentleman who listened coldly to the details of the grand dream. John, because of the decline of sterling, was not nearly so rich as Sir Otho had been; and certainly he was not prepared to lend money to a younger brother who wanted to go sailing among icebergs in search of a land of pepper and lotus flowers and gold, gold, gold. Humphrey wrote him imploring letters. He wrote him a short discourse calculated to prove that there was, that there *must* be, a north-west passage to Cathay. Then, when John remained unimpressed, he expanded upon this paper and produced his *Discourse to prove a Passage by the North west to Cataia*[1] *and East India*. At the time it was written, this *Discourse* created no remarkable stir. Humphrey Gilbert would not consent to its publication; and when John had finished with it, the *Discourse* was used only to circulate among the author's friends and

---

[1] That is, Cathay. Humphrey Gilbert, in the *Discourse,* spells it indifferently Cathay, Cathaia, and Cataia, as in the title. There was, of course, no dictionary in those times, and no fixed way of spelling any given word. Our subject's name is spelled scores of different ways, ranging from Gillbart to Jelbert. He himself always spelled it Humfrey Gylberte. Except in a few instances, where the original spelling might be considered quaint or amusing, I have modernized the spelling of all quotations contained in this volume. This, of course, does not change the sense of the quotations one whit, but it does make them much easier to read. However, at no time have I taken liberties with the original punctuation, capitalization, or paragraphing.

among merchants the author hoped to interest in his pet dream.

Apparently it was all that much wasted effort. Brother John continued cold. The merchants who had any vision at all were convinced that England's commercial salvation lay to the north-east rather than the north-west. And as for the gracious Queen, she sent Humphrey Gilbert not to America, but only to Ireland.

For once again there was trouble, and serious trouble, in Ireland. That was a better place for an excitable young captain of good blood—a better place than the library and map-room.

So he went to Ireland. But always he was dreaming of Cathay.

CHAPTER VI

SPECTACULAR SHAN O'NEIL

IT HAS been asserted by epigrammatic playwrights and novelists and the like, and perhaps with more feeling by overworked British statesmen, that there always has been and always will be an Irish question. This is not strictly correct. There was no Irish question —so far as England was concerned—before there were ships big enough to brave the open ocean instead of hugging the shores or cruising the more sheltered inland seas. Looked at from Queen Elizabeth's point of view, which was also Humphrey Gilbert's, Ireland was a nuisance and a menace. The English, then, when the Irish question was coming into existence, did not desire the Emerald Isle because it was profitable: it was anything but that: it was costly. They did not desire it because they sought glory: there could be no glory in subjugating a pack of half-naked savages, not numerous, not united, and badly armed. No, it was necessary that Ireland be under England's thumb, then and for many years afterward, only for sweet safety's sake.

This does not mean that the Irish themselves threatened the security of the larger island. The Irish were altogether too busy killing one another to think of taking the time and trouble of crossing the waters for the purpose of killing any foreigners—even if such an invasion had been conceivable for an uncivilized and highly unorganized people. But the coast of Ireland abounds in little bays and shelters quite sufficiently large for the ships of those days, which would and did harbor pirates of all sorts. Spain might find those bays convenient; France might find them so; any enemy of England might use them as ideal shoving-off places for an army of invasion. England could not get rid of this neighboring island by *wishing* it away; she could not sink it to the bottom of the sea, or shove it over to the other side of the ocean. The only thing she could do, for her own safety, was take Ireland and keep it—before some other nation got it. Irishmen might not approve of this ratiocination, but the law of self-preservation worked with the same inevitability then as always before and since.

So much for the English side of the argument. The Irish side, to be sure, is much more difficult to learn, by reason of the fact that the Irish were then, generally, an illiterate people. Who was there, when the Americans were pushing the red Indians out of the lands they had held and hunted for centuries—who was there to speak for the red Indians? It was the same with the Irish. The Spaniards, the French, perhaps, would spend money there, would give encouragement and sometimes material assistance to uprisings against the English rule; but the Spaniards and French were acting from no altruistic motives when they behaved in this fashion; like England, they were interested in Ireland, but not at all in the Irish as a people. Indeed, nobody was interested in the Irish as a people then—not even the Irish.

The spectacular Shan O'Neil, most powerful and most picturesque of all the current Irish clan leaders, precipitated the uprising Humphrey Gilbert was sent to help put down. He had visited London to argue for his rights, as he interpreted them. He had been promised safe entrance and exit, and the letter of that promise was kept. In London he was molested by nothing more serious than pop-eyed sightseers all agasp at his barbaric splendour, his barefooted kerns and gallowglasses with their long hair and long beards and their saffron shirts, and his own imposing figure. Shan probably enjoyed that part of it. A magnificent specimen of manhood, he was the father of more children than anybody ever cared to count, and with the utmost amiability he recognized all of them, invariably accepting the mother's word concerning their paternity. He loved display. He took a childish delight in the sensation he created in comparatively effete London town.

But the Queen was different. The Queen was enormously interested in and amused by him, and gaped quite as frankly as her subjects. But she didn't let that interfere with politics. She never let anything interfere with politics.

They had promised Shan O'Neil that if he came to England he would not be injured, nor would any of his followers be injured. They could come in safety and depart in safety. But *when* they could depart had not been stipulated by a wily Queen. O'Neil found himself politely a prisoner. Nobody hurt him; but the fact remained that he could not leave the country without Elizabeth's permission, and if he ever expected to see his beloved Ireland again he must first consent to Elizabeth's arrangements, which in effect would strip him of all his real hereditary power. He consented, eventually, and then he was allowed to go.

This, at least, is Shan O'Neil's story; and it has a ring of truth, though the man was often enough a shameless liar. Such tricks were characteristic of Elizabeth, of the age. Shan O'Neil had been bilked in the most approved manner; it was all quite orthodox; but that didn't make him any the less resentful. Once back on his native heath, he repudiated his vows made in London on the ground that they had been virtually forced out of him. He drew his sword and summoned his clansmen to war. "Ulster is mine and shall be mine," said Shan O'Neil. And the fight was on.

The Earl of Sussex, who had been governing Ireland for the Queen, had made the customary mess of his job, and most of what his soldiers had left had been ruined when the Butlers and the Geraldines fell to fighting one another again.

Elizabeth appointed Sir Henry Sidney to succeed Sussex. Sir Henry didn't want that assignment at all. He did everything he could to escape from it, even offering Lord Burghley a handsome bribe. He knew that it would probably bankrupt him. He would be expected to pay the soldiers himself; and though the crown was supposed to reimburse him, it was altogether likely that the crown would do so only in part, if at all. For Elizabeth had an unpleasant habit of getting rid of debts by the simple process of ignoring them; and men who would gladly charge an entrenched army, or cross the turbulent and uncharted ocean in a cockleshell, shrank before the prospect of dunning the Defender of the Faith.

But Sir Henry might squirm and wriggle and plead and bribe all he pleased. The Queen had decided that he should go to Ireland, and to Ireland he went. And one of the captains of the army that followed or accompanied him was Humphrey Gilbert. This was in December of 1565.

Ireland was a blackened desert. Here is Sir Henry's own description of the place as he found it:

"A man might ride twenty or thirty miles nor ever find a house standing, and the miserable poor were brought to such wretchedness that any stony heart would have rued the same. Out of every corner of the woods and glens they came creeping forth upon their hands, for their legs could not bear them; they looked like anatomies of death; they spoke like ghosts crying out of their graves; they did eat the dead carrions, happy when they could find them; yes, they did eat one another soon after, inasmuch as the very carcasses they spared not to drag out of their graves; and if they found a plot of watercresses or shamrocks, there they flocked as to a feast for a time."

Sir Henry was the father of Sir Philip Sidney, the poet. He was a quiet, earnest man, intelligent, well-meaning, and surely more tender-hearted than the sort of lord-lieutenant Elizabeth usually sent to the Emerald Isle. Moreover, he had known previous service in Ireland, under Sussex.

"Yet were they not at all long to continue therewithal," his description continues, "so that in short space there were none almost left, and a most populous and plentiful country was suddenly left void of man and beast; yet surely in all that war there perished not many by the sword, but all by the extremity of the famine which they themselves had wrought."

Nor was he at all happy about the English garrison he found within the Pale. "The soldiers were worse than the people," he wrote, "so beggarlike that it would abhor a general to look at them." Poorly clad, entirely unpaid, improperly supplied with provisions, they were obliged to pillage the surrounding countryside in order to remain alive—and the pickings, it will be understood, were not plentiful.

It will be understood also that Humphrey Gilbert probably was not pleased about this Irish assignment in the first place. Anyway, once there, he did everything possible to get back to England.

Less than four months after he had landed in Ireland, after a stormy passage from Bristol, his immediate superior, Colonel Edward Randolph, led a force of Englishmen against Shan O'Neil at Lough Foyle. The clan chief, surprised, was badly beaten: his band was dispersed and he himself was driven back beyond the Pale. In the confusion of the pursuit, Colonel Randolph was struck by a stray bullet—presumably fired by one of his own men, for the Irish had few, if any, firearms—and he died soon afterward.

Humphrey Gilbert had been in the fight, and as the most promising and best connected captain under Randolph he was logically the person to be appointed to the command of the regiment. Instead, he was sent back to England with dispatches telling about the victory.

Now it seems altogether likely that he himself had manipulated to get this messenger assignment. He was too important a man, and too competent a soldier, to be wasted as a dispatch-bearer—even as the bearer of dispatches about so decisive a victory as Lough Foyle. Besides, it is significant that he had with him, ready for presentation to the Queen, a petition begging her for permission to undertake a voyage to Newfoundland in search of a north-west passage to Cathay. Not for an instant had he lost sight of his ambition to blaze a short trail to India, immortality, and untold wealth.

The petition was denied. Perhaps this was partly due to the fact that Gilbert asked too much. He asked the Queen, without any security, to lend him two good ships; he asked for one-tenth of all the lands he discovered; he asked to be appointed governor of all those lands for life; and he asked for trade and fishing monopolies along the north-west passage he was to find. Elizabeth had just renewed the charter of the Merchant Adventurers, who were now incorporated as the Fellowship of English Merchants for the Discovery of New Trades; and since Gilbert's petition, if granted, would seem to infringe upon the rights of that company, Elizabeth was able to get rid of the matter by the simple expedient of turning it over to the company for an opinion.

The men who controlled the Fellowship of English Merchants, of which Gilbert himself was a member, at this time were enthusiastic about the possibility of discovering a north-*east* rather than a north-*west* passage to India. The great Sebastian Cabot, now dead, but whose word still was held in veneration by these men, had pronounced in favour of the north-east passage; and previous attempts to find such a passage at least had resulted in some Russian trade. So the Fellowship of English Merchants, though warmly protesting their respect for their distinguished young fellow member, advised the Queen against granting the petition. And the Queen, who probably never had intended to grant it anyway, accepted their advice.

It is altogether probable that Elizabeth never even read the petition. Certainly she never gave it serious thought. This Cathay her dreaming subjects were forever talking about was inestimably remote; and Humphrey Gilbert was too good a soldier, too faithful and useful a subject, and too likable a man personally, to be wasted in ocean bottoms on the other side of the world. So she sent him back to Ireland.

She was kind. She always regarded him affectionately, as an old-time friend and companion; and now she wrote to Sidney, informing that she was sending Humphrey Gilbert back on "special service," and saying some commendatory things about the young courtier. Nevertheless, she did send him back.

He was appointed a colonel. He was twenty-eight years old now, tall, well built, with a strong but refined face—a somewhat sad face—weak, dark eyes, dark hair, a soft, short beard inclined to be curly, and a "cholericke" complexion. Thus he was when, sighing, he returned to the hated task of slaughtering Irishmen.

CHAPTER VII

THE COUSINS CAUSE TROUBLE

IF THE business must be undertaken, there was no good reason why it should not somehow be made lucrative. Who it was who conceived the plan to populate considerable portions of Ireland with Englishmen prepared, as Elizabeth put it, to yield to the crown "both due obedience and reasonable yearly revenue," is not certain. Perhaps it was Humphrey Gilbert himself. He, at least, was prominent in all early discussions of the plan, which developed about the time of his first return to Ireland. And the proposed colonists, who would endeavour to keep Ireland quiet and at the same time develop a trade with England, thereby making money for all concerned—except, of course, the Irish themselves—were all Gilbert's relatives: Peter Carew, Arthur Champernoun, Richard Grenville, Warham St. Leger, buccaneers of the old school, aristocratic roughnecks.

It must not be supposed that, because Humphrey Gilbert could dream of glory and adventure and the gaining of new knowledge, he was above schemes for making money. He and his friends and relations were in a constant scramble for gold. The decline of land values in Devonshire, as elsewhere in England, had caused previously peaceful knights and squires to take to the sea; but even at sea it was difficult to recapture wealth, for the Italian states and Spain had the Mediterranean trade well in hand, Spain was lord of all the Americas, and Portugal was not prepared to brook any opposition in the exploitation of Africa. The Cham of the

Tartars had refused the English permission to transport merchandise through his lands to and from India. Chancellor, Willoughby, and Jenkinson had found the Muscovites tolerably friendly, but Russia was a bleak, far nation, difficult of access even in favourable seasons.

All the blue blood in the world will not keep a man warm in winter. You can't eat quarterlings. Moreover, these Devonshire gentlemen were intensely jealous of their ancient power, and reluctant to see that pass into the hands of upstarts who dazzled the Queen with their wealth. Elizabeth was peculiarly susceptible to wealth; and for all the fulminations of the feudal-minded, gold was more than ever a political asset. This fact rankled in Norman bosoms. Take the men who were ruling England, for instance: Walsingham's grandfather had been a brewer, his great-grandfather a cobbler; Cecil's grandfather had been a small merchant; and as for Leicester! the less said about even the *father* of that perfumed male Pompadour from nowhere, the better.

So the relatives of Humphrey Gilbert put their heads together, and emerged from conference with a typical scheme of the times—a scheme which had the approval of Elizabeth, since it involved no outlay of money on her part, and promised, even, the "reasonable yearly revenue" about which she was so anxious.

Sir Arthur Champernoun, an uncle, went to Ireland shortly after Humphrey Gilbert's return there, chiefly to talk the scheme over with this promising scion. He bore with him letters from Cecil to Sidney, endorsing the plan to turn over all confiscated lands in Munster to the Devonshire "undertakers."

Early the following year, which was 1568, this group formally petitioned Elizabeth for all these lands, and as well for all the havens and islands between Ross and the Sound of Blaskely, including the fishing rights in all adjacent waters. They offered to pay her a regular yearly rental, and £200 for the fishing monopoly; in addition, they would keep all Irishmen quiet on the land, and handle the pirates in those waters. They should certainly know how to handle the pirates, for most of them were pirates themselves—only they had a prettier name for it.

Exactly what became of this petition is not clear. Unlike the petition Humphrey Gilbert had presented, for permission to explore Newfoundland in search of a north-west passage, it was, since it concerned immediate revenue, certain of a serious reception from Her Majesty. This makes even more curious the lack of evidence concerning its disposition.

For the time, at any rate, the matter hung fire. And Humphrey Gilbert, as loyal to his Devonshire cousins as he was to his temperamental monarch, went on butchering Irishmen.

A few examples of the way he behaved in Ireland would be appropriate. But first it is only fair to point out again that the Irish at this time were without any real leaders, without any military organization, mostly without food, almost entirely without firearms. They fought with clubs, with hatchets, with anything that was available, up to and including their fists and feet and teeth. These were poor weapons with which to meet the trained English regulars in open combat. When they had obtained modern killing instruments, and learned how to use them, the Irish repeatedly showed that they were able at least to hold their own against an equal or a larger force. Nobody ever has denied their native courage and ferocity. But courage and ferocity are not sufficient for the winning of battles; and at the time Humphrey Gilbert was engaged in subjugating them the Irish were worth very little in the field even when they outnumbered their disciplined enemies four or five to one. Bearing this in mind, observe our hero:

At Knockfergus, with 150 foot soldiers behind him, he withstood 4,000 wild kerns and 60 horsemen. Two hundred Irishmen were killed or wounded, and the English, if they did not advance, at least did not retreat.

At Kilkenny, with exactly thirteen retainers, cut off from the rest of his forces, Colonel Gilbert deliberately charged 1,200 Irishmen. His black horse was wounded in eight places, his armor was dented, but he himself fought his way through to safety without a scratch.

At Kilmallock, on September 13, 1569, he held a ford single-handed, covering a retreat. He faced and fought "above twenty" mounted Irishmen; he unhorsed two of them, killed one, wounded six, and got his men over the ford safely. And again, miraculously, he came out without a single wound. "Where the Irish wondered so much they made sundry songs and Rhymes of him and his black curtal horse," relates the chronicler of this incident, "imagining himself to have been an enchanter that no man could hurt, riding on a Devil."[1]

He was answerable, under Elizabeth, only to Sir Henry Sidney. And here is what Sidney had to report to the Queen about this young man's efficiency:

"For the Colonel [Gilbert] I cannot say enough. The highways are now made free where no man might travel undespoiled. The gates of the cities and towns are now left open, where before they were continually shut or

[1] Our sole authority for these three paragraphs is Captain John Ward, who served under Colonel Gilbert at all the fights mentioned. However, there is no evidence that Ward was a relative or was otherwise interested in Gilbert's career; and the two letters from which this information is gleaned—both written to Cecil, one September 26, 1569, from Kilmallock, the other October 18th of the same year, from Limerick—do not indicate that he was a toady. There is, anyway, ample information of a general nature to substantiate these specific statements. Humphrey Gilbert and his black horse, as Captain Ward relates, became a myth in Ireland.

THE COUSINS CAUSE TROUBLE 45

guarded with armed men. There was none that was a rebel of any force but has submitted himself, entered into bond, and delivered hostages, the arch-rebel James FitzMaurice only excepted, who is become a bush-beggar, not having 20 knaves to follow him, and yet this is not the most or the best that he hath done; for the estimation that he hath won to the name of Englishmen there, before almost not known, exceedeth all the rest; for he in battle brake so many of them, where he showed how far our soldiers in valour surpassed these rebels, and he in his own person any man he had. The name of an Englishman is more terrible now to them than the sight of a hundred was before. For all this I had nothing to present him with but the honour of knighthood, which I gave him."

And so (it was on January 1, 1570) he became *Sir* Humphrey Gilbert—not because he dreamed of the glorification of England, not because he sought to open up a new world, not because he desired to found an empire in the name of his Queen and make his nation the greatest nation on earth; he became a knight not because he was eager always to add to the sum of human knowledge; no, he became a knight because he knew how to kill more Irishmen in less time than anybody else. And though Irishmen, quite understandably, may not care much for the hero of this book, Irishmen, and others as well, cannot deny that as a soldier he did a hard job well.

The butchery was by no means finished. Indeed, it was barely begun. Peter Carew and his cousins arrived in Ireland shortly before the accolade had been conferred upon their relative. They arrived bag and baggage and servants; and instantly there was renewed trouble. The very presence of this crew upon any scene —particularly the presence of Sir Peter, who seems to have been a ringleader of the lot and certainly was its oldest and most truculent member—was a guaranty of imminent disturbance.

They had some sort of vague claim to certain lands in Munster. The matter is very obscure. Apparently they did not have an official title, a legal title. Certainly —unless many papers have been lost or destroyed, and others altered—Queen Elizabeth had not *formally* sanctioned their plan to colonize Munster. It seems most likely that they had some sort of secret understanding with Her Majesty, whereby she would be clear of all responsibility for the venture if anything went wrong, yet free to accept her share of the profits if all went well. She was fond of such understandings. It is also possible that, impatient of her delays, the Devonshire thugs decided that possession was nine points of the law, and that if they went ahead and took what they wanted, and made it pay, Elizabeth probably could be induced to consent to the venture as an afterthought. In either case, they were surely bearing in mind the important fact that the governor of Munster, the strong man of Ireland, was their own young cousin and fellow Devonshire gentleman, Colonel Humphrey Gilbert. He could be counted upon to stick to the family.

Of course the Irish landowners, who were forcibly dispossessed, objected with violence. They fell upon Carew and his retainers, and there was a gay killing, from which Sir Peter himself somehow escaped. In retaliation, the probably unethical Englishmen swept down upon Sir Edward Butler's house and premises, razed the buildings to the ground, and put to the sword, after the manner of the times, every Irish man, woman, and child they could find anywhere in the neighbourhood.

Immediately all Munster was ablaze again, and Humphrey Gilbert, who had just managed to get the place quiet, had to go back to work.

He probably never hesitated. As between the claims of his own family, howsoever hazy, and the indignant clamouring of a whole nation, there would be, to him, but one possible choice. This is not meant to be derogatory to Humphrey Gilbert. It is merely an excellent illustration of the way he thought and felt about things.

CHAPTER VIII

THE QUALITY OF MERCY

SO AGAIN he had a rebellion to put down. He did it, very sensationally, in record time. This, in his own words,[1] was his method:

"I refused to parley or to make peace with any rebels, neither have I received any upon protection without his humble submission presently swearing them to be true to the Queen's Majesty, and taking bonds and pledges of them for keeping of Her Highness' peace, never practising directly or indirectly to bring in any rebels, for that I would not have them to think that the Queen's Majesty had more need of their service than they had of her mercy, neither that we were afraid of any number of them our quarrel being good, putting also all those from time to time to the sword that did belong, fed, accompany or maintain any outlaws or traitors. And after my first summoning of any castle or fort, if they would not presently yield it, I would not afterward take it of their gift but win it per force, how many lives so ever it cost, putting man, woman, and child of them to the sword, neither did I spare any malefactor unexecuted that came to my hands in any respect, using all those that I had protected with all courtesy and friendship, refusing to take any gift of any man lest my friendship should have been thought more hurtful unto them than my malice, neither did I make strange to infringe the pretended liberties of any city or town incorporate, not knowing their charters, to fur-

[1] In a letter written by Humphrey Gilbert to Cecil, December 6, 1569, from Limerick.

ther the Queen's Majesty's service, answering them that the Prince had a regular and absolute power, and that which might not be done by the one I would do by the other in cases of necessity. Being for my part constantly of this opinion that no conquered nation will ever yield willingly their obedience for love but rather for fear."

Small wonder that, as Ward put it, the enemy accounted him "more like a devil than a man, and are so afraid of him that they did leave and give up 26 castles."

"I think," the awed captain adds, "they will not now defend any castles against him."

He had protested, when appointed governor of Munster, that he was incapable of fulfilling the duties of that post. Earnestly he had begged to be relieved of the position, "knowing my insufficientories to be such, both for want of years, experience, and all other virtues necessary for such an officer."

This, understand, was no pose of modesty; it was no letter written for popular consumption and calculated to demonstrate that the gentle knight was devoid of bragadoccio, but was made of the humble stuff of heroes. It was a letter written, not to the Queen herself, but to Cecil, the cautious, realistic Lord Treasurer, the last man in the world to be deceived by talk about "insufficientories."

Presumably Humphrey Gilbert was honestly sorry, at the time of his appointment, that he had been so good a soldier. The honour was comparatively trifling. The pay was good as military pay goes—he was given, on paper, one pound a day as a colonel, eight shillings as a pettitcaptain, and four shillings as a captain of kerns, a total of one pound and twelve shillings a day in an age when sterling had at least fifteen times its present normal value. But that was little enough for a man who was dreaming in terms of millions. Moreover, it was altogether likely that he would never collect most of this money, if he collected any of it; and meanwhile his expenses were staggering. In the letter quoted above he complains that he was so poor that he was obliged to act as his own secretary, and asks again to be recalled. He was forever asking to be recalled. He didn't like Ireland any more than Ireland liked him.

In 1568 he was back in England for a short time, either because he had been wounded or was ill. But when he had recovered he was sent to Ireland again. Elizabeth, with unwonted solicitude, wrote to Sir Henry Sidney that he was to be well cared for because she considered him "toward and well able to serve us not only in that place whereof he hath charge, but of some better, if any such place there were made, whereunto he might be preferred." Pleasant words from a queen so notoriously parsimonious of praise; but the fact remained that he was ordered back to Ireland.

On July 12th of the following year he wrote to Cecil from Dublin, asking again to be allowed to return, this time "for the recovery of my eyes." A little later he wrote another letter complaining of his eyes, and begging for a recall. And finally he asserted that unless he were recalled he would go totally blind. He was recalled.

He sailed from Dublin on January 24, 1570. His eyes were suddenly cured and he was a happy man. In his purse was a letter from Sir Henry Sidney to Cecil, requesting that the money owing to Gilbert be paid him. The departing knight had spent £3,315 and 7 shillings for 100 "harquebusiers on horseback" and 200 foot soldiers, for about nine months; and he had received only £60 of this.

He was fortunate to have received that much. At least, Lord Treasurer Cecil seemed to think so. Cecil, faced with a bill for the balance, backed by Sidney's letter, took the matter under advisement. But Humphrey Gilbert had been obliged to pay cash.

It is on record that six years later he still was trying to get that money. Whether or not he ever did get it we do not know.

But he had only a short holiday. Evidently Munster could not get along without him. He had no sooner departed—he had not even reached England—when "the arch-rebel" (and first-class fighting-man) James FitzMaurice came back within the Pale, sword in hand, and such Irishmen as had shown the temerity to support the English invaders were emphatically hanged. Rebellion had begun all over again. FitzMaurice was a hard man to keep down.

Humphrey Gilbert did find time, however, to get married in England. Anne Ager is an indistinct figure. We are told that she was lovely. We *know* that she was wealthy. We know also that she was the daughter of a Kentish knight, Sir Anthony Ager of Otterden, commander of the English forces at Calais, who had been killed in the vain defense of that seaport, "preferring to die rather than join those who betrayed the city." But of the details of the courtship and marriage, and of the subsequent married life, we know nothing. It is a safe guess that Anne Ager Gilbert was not a very happy woman. This energetic husband of hers was too busy to spend much time at home, and babblings about the wonders of India are scant solace to a woman who longs for a little domestic affection.

At any rate, soon after the marriage he was sent back to Ireland. He continued to study navigation and to dream about that north-west passage. He perfected his *Discourse*, which, though it failed to stir brother John toward his money-bags, was beginning to create something of a sensation among those progressives who were interested in things far away. And he met and talked with Martin Frobisher.

Frobisher was a blond, blue-eyed giant from Yorkshire. Nautically he was the opposite of Humphrey Gilbert. That is, he was one of the best practical seamen in the kingdom and quite capable of guiding a ship through the fiercest blows of the north Atlantic, but he was almost illiterate; his paper knowledge of the art he practised was almost nil, and he had, so far as we know, dreamed no dreams at all about north-west passages to lands of gold—before he met Humphrey Gilbert.

Frobisher at this time was assigned to chase pirates from the vicinity of Ireland, and it was in Ireland that he met Sir Humphrey, who was always willing to talk with seafaring men. Sir Humphrey talked so much and so eloquently to Frobisher that the stolid Yorkshire man himself conceived the idea of sailing north of Newfoundland and discovering that passage to fame and opulence.

An obstinate person, this Frobisher—slow to get an idea, slower still to relinquish it. What he did is history. Why he did it likewise is history: his inspiration was Humphrey Gilbert; nobody can question it.

They must have been a curious pair—the dainty, determined aristocrat, with his perfectly trimmed beard, his classic education, his impeccable manners, and the hulking, silent, slow-thinking giant, who in court was the veriest boor, but on the quarterdeck was the coolest, steadiest, most skilful of men.

There is one more picture of Sir Humphrey Gilbert before, happily, we can take him away from Ireland. The authority is the poet, Thomas Churchyard; and while it may be that a poet is rarely a good authority, Churchyard, as it happens, was not constructing rhymes when he described Humphrey Gilbert, nor was he striving to malign the knight; on the contrary, he was apologizing for him, defending him.

The Gilbertian system of invariably offering the Queen's pardon to all within, before attacking any castle or fort, but refusing to extend the slightest show of mercy if that offer were refused, Churchyard praises as in the end merciful. After a time, the poet points out, nobody dared to resist him, but they "yielded without blows, bloodshed, or loss either to their party or his." And also: "It gave him such expedition in his services as that thereby he recovered more forts in one day than by strong hand would have been won in a year, and the gaining of time was one of his chiefest cares, both because he had no provision of victuals for his people, but pulled it as it were out of the enemy's mouth perforce. And also for that, his company being so small in number, not knowing how to have supplies, could not leave with the loss of men to the winning of every petty fort."

In brief, Churchyard informs us, "it made short wars." And in pursuit of this policy, the governor of Munster hit upon another quaint notion:

"His manner was that the heads of all those (of what sort soever they were) which were killed in the day should be cut off from their bodies, and brought to the place where he encamped at night, and should there be laid on the ground by each side of the way leading to his own tent, so that none could come into his tent for any cause but commonly he must pass through a line of heads, which he used *ad terrorem*, the dead feeling nothing the more pains thereby" [our poet adds, compassionately]; "and yet did it bring greater terror to the people, when they saw the heads of their dead fathers, brothers, children, kinsfolk and friends, lie on the ground before their faces as they came to speak with the said Colonel.

"Which course may by some be thought cruel, in excuse whereof it is answered, That he did but then begin that order with them, which they had in effect ever to fore toward the English. And further that he was out of doubt, that the dead felt no pains by cutting off their heads. . . ."

Gentle Humphrey Gilbert.

CHAPTER IX

HOME LIFE, DEBATES, MAGIC

THE Gilberts probably lived some of the time at Compton, some of the time at Greenway with brother John; but most of the early part of their married life, we know, they spent at a place much more convenient to the city, where Sir Humphrey was busying himself with many activities. This was Lime Hurst, or Lime Host, which name was even then being corrupted to "Lime House." It was out in the country when the Gilberts lived there. Today, as everybody knows, it is a part of the city, a slum section.

The first child was named John; evidently that was a family custom. The second was named after the father, Humphrey Jr. The third, Otho, died in Belgium. The fourth, Arthur, was killed at the siege of Amiens. The fifth was Anthony, and how he came to his end we do not know. The sixth was named Raleigh, and it was he who eventually inherited the family estates and from whom the present family is descended. There was also a daughter.

The narrative becomes a bit vague at this point; but there is evidence that Humphrey Gilbert was by no means idle during the time he lived at Lime Hurst—roughly, from 1573 to 1578.

In March of 1571 he was again in Ireland—though in what capacity it is not clear. He did not stay there long, anyway; for he was an active member of the House of Commons during Elizabeth's fourth Parliament, which was in session from April 2nd to May 29th of that year. He represented Plymouth, where he or his older brother owned considerable property. His fellow M.P. from that seaport was Sir William Hawkins.

Again, in Parliament, Humphrey Gilbert was always the courtier. Elizabeth was right, invariably. Whoever said that she could possibly be wrong was a traitor and no patriot. This particular Parliament was heavily Puritan and inclined to be independent, exacerbating the Queen, and making her ardent champion Sir Humphrey an unpopular figure in its debates. When it was proposed to interfere with the Queen's plan to grant a salt monopoly to certain Bristol merchants, Sir Humphrey made loud and long objection. Parliament had no *right* to interfere with monopolies, which were and always had been a royal prerogative. He was very hot about it. Trying to tamper with one of the Queen's privileges, he said, was in effect denying that the woman really was Queen at all—and surely *that* was nothing less than treason! He hinted that the House would do well to mind its own business and not strain too far the royal tolerance.

Nothing was said about the monopoly matter for a few days after that. Then Peter Wentworth made answer; and the answer was harder, harsher, more outspoken than the speech which had provoked it. It must not be supposed, either, that this Wentworth was any political hothead seeking but applause. Wentworth was a staunch and true defender of the rights of Parliament, who repeatedly had the courage to oppose the Queen when he thought she was going beyond her power, and who was twice thrown into the Tower for his impertinence; he died in the Tower.

He likened Sir Humphrey now to a chameleon, capable of changing itself to any color except white. "He is a flatterer, a liar, and a naughty man," shouted Wentworth.

Gilbert was on his feet instantly. But he could not

obtain permission to speak; three times the House refused to listen to his defense.

Nevertheless, Parliament did not interfere with Elizabeth's salt monopoly; and presumably she was grateful to Sir Humphrey, for these monopolies, admittedly evils and eventually abolished, were among her best sources of revenue.

It was a very busy Parliament, for those days. Among other things, it passed an act which made church attendance on Sunday compulsory for every person in the kingdom, and likewise made Holy Communion at least twice a year compulsory;[1] it regulated the importation of bow-staves, pointing out that "the use of Archery not only hath ever been but yet is, by God's special gift to the English nation, a singular defense to this Realm"; it forbade the drying in England of fish caught by foreigners, and passed several other acts calculated to benefit English fisherfolk; it provided a startlingly modern reforestation plan; it made it an act of high treason, punishable by death, even to discuss the question of an heir to the throne, except the same be the natural issue of her [Elizabeth's] body"; it passed a law making it compulsory for all persons in the kingdom over the age of seven years to wear every Sunday and every Holy Day a woolen cap, "knit, thicked, and dressed in England"; and finally, as its last official act, it did the only thing Elizabeth had called it into session for—that is, it granted her a subsidy of £100,000 for the conduct of the nation's business.

Her Majesty, woman-like, had the last word. In her prorogation she asserted that "some members of the Lower House . . . had forgotten their duties by wast-

[1] Elizabeth later refused to give this act her royal assent, on the ground that the Church was her own property and Parliament had no business with it. It made her furious whenever a Parliament attempted to institute changes in the Church.

ing their time in superfluous speech, and had meddled with matters not pertaining to them, nor within the capacity of their understanding." This "audacious folly," she said, deserved her "severest censure."

But Humphrey Gilbert was not one of those rebuked. He had done his work well, and his reward took the form of an appointment, in letters-patent dated June 25, 1571, as Surveyor-general of "all horses, Armour, weapons, munitions, artillery, etc.," throughout England "for seven years next ensuing." At the end of that time it was renewed for another seven years.

Whether this position was as important as it sounds we do not know. It may have been a sinecure. The feudal laws requiring certain knights and noblemen to keep on hand for call from the Crown a specified number of men-at-arms with their equipment and weapons, were being ignored; and the post of Surveyor-general of all horses, Armour, weapons, etc., was created for the purpose of enforcing these laws, or else, more practically, for the purpose of collecting fines for their violation. No salary went with the position. Elizabeth rarely paid her servants; she expected them to make their work lucrative by methods which were not then considered graft. However, a legitimate revenue was provided for the new official, who was to receive three-fifths of the money collected in fines—the balance, of course, going to the Queen. Section Four of the letters-patent conferring the position upon Sir Humphrey and defining his duties and powers, specifically provides that "for the better answering of the money coming to her Majesty" through these fines, the amounts collected should be written into bills signed by Sir Humphrey and a certain number of the six assistant commissioners authorized, and certified in the Exchequer. Sir Humphrey was obliged to enter into a bond in the Court of the Exchequer to guarantee a true accounting. Elizabeth took no chances.

One of the duties imposed upon the new official was "the suppression of unlawful games, by which archery is greatly decayed." This solicitude for the longbow, typical of the times, must not be thought to have been inspired wholly or even chiefly by patriotism. No doubt there were men who thrilled at the memory of the twanging strings at Agincourt and Crécy, and who believed that England's future safety lay in these weapons. No doubt, too, there were old-fashioned military leaders who had little use for the clumsy muskets which were increasing in armies all over Europe. Then, the longbow was more dependable than the musket; it could be discharged much more rapidly, and was, therefore, more effective in stopping a cavalry charge; it would kill at the same distance, or even at a greater distance if the wind were right; it would penetrate armor almost as well; and finally it was a cleaner, lighter, more likable, infinitely less expensive weapon.

But the principal reason for the attempts to stimulate archery by law was a commercial one. England always had been celebrated for her longbows, the best in the world. It was a considerable trade; and the coming of the musket was hurting it. The best makers of firearms were Italian. The greatest armourers and swordmakers were Italian or Spanish. The march of progress was costing English manufacturers a lot of money; and they supposed, as men always have, that the march of progress could be brought to a halt by legislation. Humphrey Gilbert was expected to help them recover their pristine prosperity.

How hard he worked at this job we have no means of knowing. We do know that his appointment caused many murmurs of jealousy; and we also know that, however much money the appointment might have brought him, it was not enough to finance the project upon which his heart still was set. He had sufficient to take his place in Court as a gentleman, to glitter with tolerable brilliancy, and to keep himself surrounded by servants and retainers. He did not have sufficient—not nearly sufficient—to take to the ocean as admiral of his own fleet. His persistence is amazing. Once he had conceived a plan to colonize North America and use this colony as a base for the seeking of a north-west passage—for the dream had grown to this, by now—nothing could swerve him, nothing could make him forget.

In 1572 he petitioned Elizabeth for a large grant of land in southeastern Ireland, probably hopeful of building a big fishing business there and so finally managing to get the money he desired. Elizabeth still owed him a considerable sum for his expenses in Ireland. It seems like little enough he was asking. But the petition was not granted.

Then he turned to alchemy, permitting Sir Thomas Smyth to interest him in the Meadley experiments.

Nowadays, it seems rather silly; and the biographer is embarrassed to see his subject dabbling in such nonsense, and is tempted to avoid mention of it. Still, it happened. And it is worth mention at the outset, that Sir Thomas Smyth was not a wild-eyed visionary, but a hard-headed man of business; and that the other two persons interested in Meadley—the Earl of Leicester and William Cecil, who had only just been created Lord Burghley—were likewise known, and particularly Burghley, for their caution in such matters. They were all well-educated, well-read men of affairs.

William Meadley said that he could transmute iron, which was plentiful and cheap in England, into copper, which was both rare and expensive. He said he could do this by means of vitriol. He performed his process at

Smyth's London house, and evidently convinced that personage that it was practicable—though the original method was found to be too expensive. Smyth interested his three friends, and they agreed to finance Meadley. They incorporated into "The Society of the New Art," and they were very mysterious about it, very earnest. Smyth and Humphrey Gilbert gave Meadley £100 cash, and they rented for him, at £300 a year, some of Lady Mountjoy's property, which the alchemist said contained the ingredients necessary for his work.

Then Smyth was sent to Paris, as Elizabeth's ambassador, replacing Francis Walsingham; and Humphrey Gilbert was expected to oversee Meadley's work.

He promptly fell out with the miracle-worker. What he said to Meadley we do not know, but evidently he suffered one of those fits of temper he sometimes had, for Meadley's letters to other members of the Society of the New Art complain that he had been "scorched with ill repute" and speak of "Mr. Gilbert's malice and foul play." He would be "scorched" indeed if Sir Humphrey lost his temper with him. For Sir Humphrey, ordinarily quiet and mild-mannered, sometimes flew into a fit of rage and made things very warm for everybody in sight.

He withdrew in disgust. Burghley and Leicester appear to have done the same, perhaps as a result of something Gilbert told them. Smyth, on his return from France, for a time continued his interest in Meadley and the transmutation hocus-pocus, in which he appears to have kept faith; but eventually he, too, withdrew. Meadley seems to have found difficulty in locating other financial backers as gullible as these. Two years later he was in an English jail as a debtor, and that is the last we hear about *him*.

No richer, then, but poorer, and with Cathay seemingly farther away than ever, Humphrey Gilbert turned wearily back to his old business of fighting. Unofficially, irregularly, but at the secret command of the Queen, he crossed the Channel at the head of 1,500 men to help the Dutch rebels throw off the terrible yoke of Spain.

CHAPTER X

A THANKLESS JOB

EVEN in those days, all wars were wars of defense only. And as far as Elizabeth was concerned, they weren't wars at all. She didn't like wars. They cost too much money. The only thing she would tolerate, in emergencies, was what she herself accurately termed "underhand war." For one reason, that could be carried on largely at somebody else's expense; and for another, she was never obliged to take responsibility for it.

The sort of war in which Humphrey Gilbert now was engaged was, from his and from Elizabeth's point of view, an "underhand war." It does not make a very pretty picture—though there are historians who have tried to touch it up with the suggestion that Elizabeth was valiantly defending Protestantism and assisting the persecuted, embattled Dutchmen to regain their ancient liberties. But this is preposterous. And so is the contention that religious convictions and a desire to see fair play were similarly inspiring Sir Humphrey Gilbert when he took his 1,500 men across the Channel. Far from being any white-clad Crusader setting forth in a holy cause, he resembles, even according to the ethics of the times, something between a mediæval mercenary and a modern gang-leader. It was a sordid assignment. The Low Countries had been fought over so many times, and even now were so littered with groups of maurading, pillaging soldiers, unpaid, often unfed, always inhumanly cruel to the inhabitants, that, to quote Humphrey Gilbert's friend, George Gascoigne, it was hard to distinguish " 'twixt broyles and bloudie warres."

64 A THANKLESS JOB

The Netherlands had become Spanish because they were part of the estate Philip had inherited from his father, the emperor. Previously, they had been Austrian. They were handed over to an unsympathetic Spanish monarch (Charles V was dead now, and his son Philip was king of Spain, no longer merely prince regent) precisely as though they were that many articles of furniture the dying emperor desired to keep in the family. Containing a large Protestant population, and many lords and subjects not at all prepared to surrender their riches and privileges to a pinched, weak-kneed person on the Peninsula, they gave Philip more trouble than all his other possessions put together—and Philip at this time, or a little later, owned outright about half of the world, more than any one person has owned since or before. Philip would have saved himself a vast expenditure of time, trouble, and money if he had permitted the Dutchmen to have their freedom and be done with it. But such a thought never occurred to him; it was his *duty*, his God-conferred *duty*, to keep those provinces under his rule.

Now Philip's army was the biggest, the best organized and best equipped, the most skilfully led, in all the world. Nobody could question that. The Low Countries alone never could hope to free themselves of their Spanish masters: they were obliged to seek allies.

It was some years before Humphrey Gilbert crossed the Channel (it was, in fact, on August 6, 1571) that the English ambassador at Paris—long, spare, very serious-minded Sir Francis Walsingham—had a conversation with Count Louis of Nassau, younger brother of the exiled Prince of Orange, one of the leading Dutch rebels. This was shortly after the five-day conference King Charles IX of France had conducted, very secretly, with the same nobleman.

Walsingham liked Count Louis instantly. "I hope,"

he wrote to the Earl of Leicester, "that God hath raised him up in these days to serve for an instrument for the advancement of His glory." What he meant by this was that he hoped Count Louis and his brother would be able to defy Spain successfully. Walsingham hated Spain.

This was the count's plan, as outlined to the French monarch and the English ambassador:

France, England, and as many of the semi-independent German states as could be interested, would unite with the Dutch rebels and invade the Low Countries, driving Spain out. Then the Dutch lords would be given back their estates and other holdings; Brabant, Guelders and Luxembourg would revert to the German Empire; Flanders and Artois would go to France; and Holland and Zealand would be handed to England. And so everybody would be happy, except Spain; and Spain, with most of Europe arrayed against her, would be powerless to object.

Walsingham was, for him, downright enthusiastic. "I think it dangerous to advise a prince to wars, for that the issue of wars is doubtful," he wrote in this same letter to Leicester. "Notwithstanding, things may so fall out sometimes as nothing can be more dangerous than not to enter into wars. Wars grounded on ambition for increase of dominion are always unjust, but wars grounded on necessity, for safety's sake, are necessary."

Walsingham, parenthetically, had learned his politics in Italy. And Italian statecraft was the vogue then. Elizabeth loved it.

The count's plan seemed to the Englishman to have three great advantages, and he listed them. It would drive Spain out of the Low Countries. It would prevent France from coöperating single-handed with the Dutch rebels and so, in the end, getting too big a slice of the territory to be grabbed in this "necessary" war. And finally:

"A third mischief may be avoided of no less, or rather greater consequence, which is that those who otherwise will not perhaps live quietly at home, may be kept occupied by being employed abroad."

This third point is significant, and particularly interesting to us here. For it is true that one big reason why there was such scandalous battling in those times was the fact that there were so many hard-bitten soldiers who grew restless after a brief spell of peace; their only business was the business of war, and if they didn't have a war every now and then they were apt to get into serious trouble. A wise monarch in the sixteenth century always managed to have some sort of conflict in progress or about to break, in order that his more truculent subjects might work off their surplus energy and develop their talents for killing, in another land. It was, really, sound policy.

Walsingham knew. He was no blustering, clanking general; on the contrary, he was emphatically a man of peace. But he understood his fellow men.

This grand alliance scheme fell through. But it did result, directly, the following April, in the Treaty of Blois, by which England and France bound themselves to be better friends in the future, and secretly agreed to do as much as they thought advisable to get Spain out of the Low Countries. The Treaty of Blois was sheerly a gesture, and an empty one. So far as can be learned, not one of its provisions was kept by either party; and probably neither party ever even intended to keep them, each desiring little more than to keep the other quiet and to give Spain a good scare.

But it was significant. That always-important matter of the European balance of power was involved in it. For centuries past England and France had been ene-

A THANKLESS JOB

mies, England and Spain friends. Now Spain was getting too powerful, and England and France, though hating one another still with as lively a hatred as ever they had known, were drawing together for mutual protection.

Still, Elizabeth did not want war with Spain. Oh no! Nothing so definite as that! She would have liked a chunk of the Low Countries, preferably a seaport. She was mindful always of the fact that she officially styled herself, among other things, "Queen of France." On paper, at least, she still laid claim to a considerable portion of the adjacent mainland. Calais had been the last English possession there; and the fall of Calais had exercised a tremendous influence over the royal mind of England. It had happened just before Queen Mary died, and possibly it had hastened her death. "If they cut me open when I am dead," Mary had declared, "they will find the word 'Calais' written on my heart."

It was scarcely likely that Elizabeth could recover Calais, but she would like *one* of the ports on the other side of the Channel from England. It would enhance her prestige immeasurably. Earlier, when the Huguenots had been imploring her aid, she dickered for Havre de Grace; but in spite of the efforts of her soldiery, which included young Humphrey Gilbert, she had failed to obtain that city.

And now the Dutch rebels were dangling Flushing before her. It was bait too tempting for Elizabeth to resist.

At the same time, she was not prepared to risk an open war. Spain was powerful, and war was expensive. Elizabeth, after passing through one of those periods of mental torture, trying to make up her mind, at length hit upon the compromise of another "underhand war."

Thomas Morgan was permitted to cross the Channel

with three hundred men. This was not an English force. No, indeed! It was a gang of adventurers, desperadoes.

And Morgan was closely followed by a much greater force under Humphrey Gilbert. Again, this was no Engglish army, but merely an unauthorized rabble of bandits, mercenaries, who had somehow been recruited, equipped, disciplined, and sneaked out of the country, without the Queen being permitted to know anything about it.

Humphrey Gilbert must have understood this perfectly. He must have had many long conferences with Elizabeth on the subject, before he sailed. His instructions were to keep away from open battle if it were humanly possible, and not to risk the loss of any of his men. An elaborate code of letter-signals had been concocted—when he was told one thing, it meant another. It was all worked out, but he must keep it in his memory, for they did not dare to commit it to paper.

Most important of all, he must not forget that if he could do so without danger to the Queen's reputation, and without too much expense, he was to capture Flushing and hold it. For Flushing, after all, was the objective.

All this fuss fooled nobody highly placed. The Spaniards understood what Humphrey Gilbert was supposed to do, and when their ambassador at London protested against the expedition, it was purely as a matter of form; for the ambassador knew well enough what Elizabeth would answer. Elizabeth, be sure of it, did not disappoint him. She declared that Humphrey Gilbert had collected and trained his men, and taken them out of the country, entirely without her permission and even without her knowledge. He was a private adventurer, a pirate on land. She would not be accountable for him.

Remember, he was liable to the same treatment, if captured, as a sea pirate—that is, summary death. So were all his men. There was nothing new about this. Exactly the same situation had prevailed when Elizabeth unofficially had sent her soldiers to France to help the Huguenots in their fight for religious freedom. Any of those who had fallen prisoner to the forces under the Duke of Guise were hanged promptly, without any sort of trial; and around their necks, as warnings, had been suspended signs informing that this had been done because these men had come to France as robbers and against the wishes of the Queen of England—though Guise and his followers knew as well as everybody else that the Queen herself actually had dispatched them.

Such an assignment as this, then, required for commander a man who was either a fighting fool, willing to undertake any risk for the sake of getting into a war; or else a man who was so devoted to his Queen that he was willing to lie for her, risk his life for her, risk his *reputation* for her, and not expect reward. I think we are safe in assuming that Sir Humphrey Gilbert was a little of each.

CHAPTER XI

EXPERIMENTS IN DECEIT

ANOTHER conniving woman, Catherine de' Medicis, was ruling France. "Madame la Serpente," her youngest son called her; and there is justice in the opprobrium, however unfilial. For there was something decidedly snakelike in those tiny dark eyes which seemed the smaller because they were set in a large, bland, placid face. Certainly all the woman's movements were circuitous; she was crooked by nature; she was unable, apparently, ever to do anything straight, direct, honest; and it is small enough excuse for her that, unlike Elizabeth, she was not a reigning monarch, but only a queen mother, who was obliged to wield her power by means of a cat's-paw, her feeble-minded son, Charles IX.

Now Catherine de' Medicis was playing the same game as Elizabeth in the Low Countries, and this fact made Humphrey Gilbert's thankless task even more difficult than anybody had anticipated. For Catherine de' Medicis desired Flushing also; and when Sir Humphrey arrived in that city, early in July of 1572, he found it occupied by Huguenots ostensibly there, as he was, to assist the freedom-seeking Dutchmen in the name of the Protestant religion. These Huguenots, parenthetically, were fighting for the French crown now, not against it; for, oddly enough, there was no civil war in progress in France at the moment.

Instantly there was trouble. And only some sort of hastily-arrived-at agreement could prevent worse trouble in the very near future. Both forces were composed

EXPERIMENTS IN DECEIT

of reckless, brutal adventurers, and each thought that the other had no business to be there.

Sir Humphrey signed such an agreement with the governor and boroughmen of Flushing on July 15th, in behalf of himself and of the Frenchmen, his cocrusaders for the liberty of the Dutch. Two hundred Englishmen and a like number of Frenchmen were to be left in the city as a garrison; and if more were needed to defend the place in case of attack by the Spaniards, then equal numbers of both would be admitted; but under no circumstances were either the French or the English to control the city. It was an agreement neither side intended to respect. There was no more sincerity in it than there had been in the Treaty of Blois, signed a little earlier, by which France and England had pledged themselves to be bosom friends for the rest of all time. However, it served to prevent an immediate row.

The commander of the Dutch forces at Flushing was one t'Zaareets, and he and Humphrey Gilbert, from the very beginning, quarrelled constantly. Gilbert, in his reports—for this leader of an unofficial force was regularly sending official reports to London—complained that t'Zaareets was cowardly, jealous, troublesome. It is evident from his own letters, and from the reports of others, that Humphrey Gilbert himself was a troublesome sort of person during this campaign, too: repeatedly he lost his temper; it seems he did not like this business at all, and he was impatient of all obstacles and delays.

They agreed to make a descent upon Bruges, which they had heard was poorly garrisoned. They occupied the village of Ardenburgh—1,400 English, 400 Walloons, and 600 French. Bruges they found very well garrisoned and fortified, after all, so they shifted to Sluys. The preliminary attack was driven back and the defenders sallied forth in pursuit. Gilbert and t'Zaareets arrived in time to drive the garrison back into the city, and the commander of the defending forces consented to parley for terms of surrender. In fact, the wily Spaniard only was gaining time while he sent for reinforcements and additional supplies. The English and Dutch were neatly fooled, and when the parley was broken off and the fighting recommenced, they found themselves in no condition to take the city promptly. So they withdrew.

It is not astounding that Humphrey Gilbert, so sensational a captain in the field, showed so poorly in this sort of warfare. There was a vast difference between the general who could lead men in the field with success and the general who could hammer a city into submission. Gilbert was accustomed to sweep everything before him. He was all the open-field warrior—the reckless, dashing, have-it-out-now sort of fighter. He lacked the patience, the bulldog tenacity, the always-alert eye for details, and perhaps also the skill, to conduct a successful siege.

Shifting to Bruges, they sent a trumpeter to summon that city to surrender. The military commander, Count de Reux, impolitely replied that he'd see them all hanged before he'd surrender—and he meant exactly that.

"Sir Humphrey was then in great choler, swearing divers oaths that he would put all to the sword unless they would yield."[1]

But this was not Ireland. His bullying had no effect upon the hard-bitten Spanish veterans to whom war was an everyday business. He was faced here by well-walled,

---

[1] *The Actions of the Lowe Countries*, by Sir Roger Williams, 1618. Practically all the information on military matters contained in this chapter is from this source, the only one available. Sir Roger was a good authority, however. He was present at the various scenes he described, knew Gilbert, t'Zaareets, and Morgan personally, and so far from being a toady, was not at all pleased with the way the whole campaign was conducted, and was not afraid to say so.

well-fortified cities, defended by organized and highly
efficient soldiers every man of whom was as brutal and
fearless as he himself. Besides, the allies received word
at this time that large reinforcements were on their way
to Bruges. They retired without having struck a blow.

A few days later, slipping out of Ardenburgh, they
ambushed a convoy on the way to Bruges, killing many
Spaniards and taking much artillery and supplies. But
again came word of approaching Spanish reinforcements, so they retreated to Flushing.

On the way they crossed to the island of South Beve-
land and attacked Tergoes, which they found well defended. The advance force under Morgan was driven
back with heavy losses, and Pedro Pacheco, the commander, attempted a sally calculated to cut them all
down. Gilbert and his Dutch ally arrived in time to
drive Pacheco back. Afterward, they were censured for
not cutting off Pacheco and crushing him. Their excuse
was that they didn't know the countryside well enough
to realize that this would have been possible. But, as
our chronicler, Sir Roger, points out, they *should* have
known the countryside before they moved against the
town. That was part of their business.

Anyway, they tried to take Tergoes and failed. And
they limped back to Flushing.

There they received a shock. The inhabitants of the
city refused to open the gates for them; the inhabitants
were frankly disgusted with soldiers who could conduct
no more successful a campaign than the one just closed,
and they suggested to Gilbert and to t'Zaareets that
they go out and do something creditable before they
applied for readmission to the ancient and honorable
city of Flushing.

Humiliated, the Dutch and English occupied the village of Souburg. There a large force of Spaniards from
Middleburgh, waxing over-bold, attempted to attack

them; and they turned upon these fellows with savage ferocity, making a great slaughter and sending them back to Middleburgh in a panic.

After that, Flushing let them in.

But Humphrey Gilbert found himself getting nowhere. He knew what was expected of him; but he was aware, too, that everybody else knew this, in spite of Elizabeth's cumbersome precautions. He was supposed to hoodwink the Spanish, the Dutch, and the French, all at once; but the Spanish, the Dutch, and the French were perfectly acquainted with this fact, and were not willing to permit him to get out of their sight. Perplexed, he wrote to Burghley, asking advice.

Burghley responded by sending to the knight one Mr. Pickman, or Pyckman, "a very wise and valiant man," who bore two letters and some word-of-mouth instructions.

The letters have survived. One of them, signed by the Queen herself, peremptorily orders Humphrey Gilbert and all his men to return to England. How he was to use this command is explained in the other, longer letter.

If possible, he was to coöperate with both the Dutch and the French in some siege. Then, asserting that it had just been received, he was to produce the recall command signed by the Queen. He was to express his regrets, and depart. Ostensibly making for England, while the others continued their siege, he was suddenly to turn and fall upon Flushing. Once in that city, surely he was soldier enough to know how to keep it.

There were other instructions in this longer letter. For one thing, it had reached the ears of the Queen that some of Humphrey Gilbert's men who had fallen prisoner to the Spaniards had asserted, just before they were hanged, that they had been sent to the Low Countries by Elizabeth herself. This, of course, must be stopped; and Sir Humphrey was instructed to deny it in such a manner that his denial would reach the ears of the Duke of Alba, the supreme Spanish commander, who had complained. Sir Humphrey was to make it clear to the duke that the English were in the Low Countries not for the purpose of inciting and abetting rebellion against Spain, but, on the contrary, for the purpose of assisting their brothers, the Spaniards, to put down that very rebellion. How he was to manage this is not made clear. Perhaps the word-of-mouth instructions contained some suggestions on this point. The entire matter is so drenched with deceit that it is difficult to understand it at all.

Gilbert found himself in a tight place, in Flushing. The townspeople did not like the English, favouring rather the French, who were plotting with them, according to Sir Humphrey, to turn the English out. Sir Humphrey offered, in a letter to Burghley, to turn the tables on the French, using their own trick against them by inciting a mutiny between the townspeople and the Huguenots, and then taking the part of the townspeople. The French could be chased out, and Elizabeth would be able to explain, later, that this had been done for the benefit of the dear Dutch, whom French and English alike were endeavouring to help. He asked for instructions on this matter; but whether he ever got them we do not know, for this was scarcely the sort of thing Burghley was likely to commit to writing.

It is not improbable that Humphrey Gilbert himself was as hopelessly confused about all this as, subsequently, historians have been. In the postscript of one letter to Burghley he writes, tactfully:

"I do know that Her Majesty and My Lords of the Council are many times enforced to *pretend* that they nothing desire. Wherefore what letters soever shall be sent me from the Lords of the Council for revoking of me home, I will think them but for form, except your Honour do write me your private letters to return, and then I will with out delay, God willing, obey them, otherwise proceed here as I shall see cause."

At any rate, he returned to his previous job of trying to take Tergoes. It was an inglorious siege. Sir Humphrey and his under officer, Morgan, engaged in a bitter quarrel, and Morgan threatened to withdraw with his men; the matter was patched up somehow. Sir Humphrey and t'Zaareets, all this time, were squabbling. Reinforcements arrived from the Prince of Orange, but though they were numerous, they were raw troops and apparently more of a hindrance than a help. A breach was opened in the walls of Tergoes, and an assault was made; but it was beaten back with heavy losses.

Then an aged but spirited Spanish general, Mondragon, who was stationed at Bergen-op-Zoom, eight supposedly impassable miles away, broke the siege with dramatic abruptness. He had heard of a route by which his troops could cross the dangerous Verdronken Lands between Bergen-op-Zoom and Tergoes, and with 3,000 picked men, led by a native guide, he made a brilliant forced march, totally surprising the English and Dutch, and sending them running for their lives. It was Sir Humphrey's most ignominious defeat and it ended his campaign in the Low Countries.

Now while Sir Humphrey had been striving to juggle Flushing into English hands, the St. Bartholomew massacres were being conducted in France, and these made a radical difference in Elizabeth's attitude toward her nearest neighbour on the Continent. England once more began making eyes at Spain, for obviously England could not afford to dicker any longer with a nation which slaughtered its Protestants indiscriminately and without any warning, and obviously also England could not afford to have both France and Spain arrayed against her.

After all, England could have the friendship of Spain any time she desired it, so long as she didn't go too far with France; for Spain would rather have England as a friend than France, Philip being a Hapsburg born.

So Elizabeth made a great show of recalling Humphrey Gilbert in disgrace, informing her one-time suitor, Philip, that she was doing this as an act of friendliness to him. She beamed upon Philip, flirted with him. But Spanish spies in London reported to their king that she was only making the best of an evil necessity, and probably they were right.

Whatever the reason, Humphrey Gilbert landed in England November 5th, and went directly to Court, where he reported privately and unofficially to the Queen. She then sent him out of the city again, with instructions to make a second, public entrance. This time he must not attempt to go to Court. Instead, he must go to the homes of influential acquaintances and implore them to intercede for him with the angry Queen, to beg her forgiveness for having committed the reprehensible act of leading an English mob in the Low Countries. He was to behave like a man in disgrace, already ruined, trembling in fear of his very life, while Elizabeth simulated indignation.

All this for the benefit of the Spaniards, who were not fooled by it for an instant. But it kept the records straight. The whole colossal blunder had been conceived in deceit and in a spirit of greed mixed with timidity, and so it was fitting that it should be ended on this note.

CHAPTER XII

ANOTHER GRAND IDEA

NO SOONER was he back in England, and for all his faked "disgrace," than he was busy again with maps and plans for that north-west voyage.

Ortelius, the great Flemish cartographer, visited England at about this time, and Humphrey Gilbert conferred with him at length.

He conferred with others. With Simon Fernandez, a Portuguese pilot who had made various trips to Florida and the West Indies and who was a rare find in England, being willing to guide any ship to the Americas at an hour's notice. With Richard Hakluyt, that quiet, mild-mannered clergyman to whose researches and recordings we owe so much of our present knowledge of navigation and navigators of Elizabeth's time. With Anthony Jenkinson, who had made the north-east trip in vain but who still was convinced that England's commercial destiny lay in that direction. With burly Martin Frobisher, sea captain, who was now working as hard as Gilbert himself to promote a voyage of discovery north of Newfoundland. With Dr. John Dee, friend of Mercator, lecturer, mathematician, astrologer and astronomer, meteorologist, metallurgist, inventor, economist, big-navy agitator, author, fortune-teller, chemist, etc., etc., who was engaged in writing *General and Rare Memorials Pertaining to the Perfect Art of Navigation*. Dr. Dee was a tall, thin man with a long, pointed beard and a mysterious manner. He lived at Mortlake, an old, rambling house on the Thames, where he sat surrounded by hieroglyphics and cabalistic signs, future-showing mirrors, crystal globes, and the like, in addition to some 4,000 books and manuscripts—a tremendous collection for those days. He had cast the horoscopes of Queen Mary and the Princess Elizabeth, and was frequently consulted for star-reading and fortune-telling by great persons of the Court, sometimes by the Queen herself. Only recently he had taken an interest in navigation, apparently having turned to it after mastering every other strange science known to his time. For navigation *was* a strange science in those days. It was a thing tinged with mystery, dark and fascinating, the sort of thing proper persons would look at askance. The very fact that Dr. Dee took it up is in itself proof of this.

But the Merchant Adventurers stayed firm in their disapproval; and so long as they refused to sanction Gilbert's plan, he was helpless. The Merchant Adventurers seemed unwilling to do anything themselves about opening new sea routes; they still carried on a certain trade with Russia—this having been started by the voyages of Willoughby and Jenkinson—but they were making no effort to discover a passage to Cathay, whether north-east or north-west. Yet they held the charter for exclusive exploration rights both north-east and north-west, and without their permission Humphrey Gilbert could do nothing but make plans and recite arguments.

Balked, then, in his chief ambition, he turned in another direction. If he could not go north-west, he would go south. He was simply bursting with desire to sail uncharted seas and to plant a piece of England in some far, savage country.

Great plans were in the making. He and his Devonshire cousins and some others—but Humphrey Gilbert always was the moving spirit—desired to sail in four ships to that part of the Americas lying below the equator, and there to plant an English settlement and develop a trade with the mother country. They worked it all out. They raised the money, £5,000. They prepared, and on March 22, 1574, presented to the Queen and to Lord High Admiral Lincoln separate petitions begging for permission to make this venture, with a specification in detail attached. They were even given a dinner by the city of Plymouth in celebration of the impending expedition.

The petitions themselves are brief, asking only for the Queen's permission and her blessing, and the Lord High Admiral's approval. The attached argument is much longer, and probably was written by Humphrey Gilbert himself.

It points out that the Spaniards held the western part of the New World, the Portuguese the eastern part, and the French the northern part. Obviously, then, God had so arranged things that the southern portion should be given to England, "to whom," the memorial adds with a note of bitterness, "the others in times past have first been offered."[1]

The American lands south of the equator, it pointed out, were perhaps generally claimed by Spain, but were not *specifically* claimed by that nation, which had made no attempt to colonize there. Occupation of this part of the New World could not possibly give offense to any other nation, the petitioners assert, a trifle naïvely. Being in the southern temperate zone, it would have a climate roughly corresponding with that of England itself, and therefore it would constitute an excellent market for English woolens: evidently the purpose of the petitioners was to persuade the untamed savage to adopt London-made clothes. That the project would have divine sanction could be taken for granted, inasmuch as the colonists would teach Christianity to the savages,

---

[1] This is not further explained; but presumably it refers to the fact that Christopher Columbus offered his services to Henry VII of England before he turned to Ferdinand and Isabella of Spain.

ANOTHER GRAND IDEA

who would certainly take promptly to that enlightenment, "especially when it shall not carry with it the unnatural and incredible absurdities of Papistry."

There is no record of any English mariner at this time ever having gone south of the Spanish Main (it was three years before Drake started his voyage around the world), yet the petitioning group lists among its assets "mariners and sailors to whom the passage *almost* thither is known"; and elsewhere it refers to the "hole line and zona torrida" and asserts that "sundry of our own nation and some such as are to go in those voyages have passed it."

Evidently there was still much superstition, and in high places, too, about passing the equator. Judging from the pains the petitioners take to stress the voyages already made over that imaginary line, by Spaniards and Portuguese, they feared that those to whom they had directed their petitions might suppose that to cross the equator was to drop off the end of the world. It is quite possible.

They were practical enough about the matter. Elizabeth herself would not be asked to contribute any money or any ships, but only to give her permission for and blessing upon the enterprise. Hints of great riches, in which she would share, were dangled hopefully in front of her, and there were many protests that such a colony would not affront any Christian prince. England, not being a Catholic nation, certainly was not to consider herself bound by the fact that eighty-five years earlier a Spanish Pope had divided the New World between Spain and Portugal. Even France, though a Catholic nation, did not respect this division. Philip could not lay claim to lands his mariners had never even seen, the petitioners pointed out; and they insisted that, anyway, they would touch at no Spanish or Portuguese seaports, but would carry on all their trade direct with the mother country—that is, unless the Spaniards and Portuguese expressed a willingness to trade such as they had shown when Hawkins had approached them. The fact that Hawkins had approached them with cannon loaded and primed and aimed, and had obliged them to exchange goods whether they liked it or not, discreetly was left unmentioned.

These petitions were presented by "certain gentlemen of the West Country," including Sir Humphrey Gilbert; his cousin Sir Richard Grenville, who later became immortal for his fight with the Spaniards off the Azores; Sir George Peckham, a wealthy Roman Catholic, an old and trusted friend of Humphrey Gilbert; a Mr. Carlyle, son-in-law of Sir Francis Walsingham, Elizabeth's minister, who always was ready to encourage colonization and exploration attempts; and others. Most of them were from Devonshire, and all of them either were related to or associated with Humphrey Gilbert, their leader.

Nothing came of the scheme. The petition never was granted. We do not know whether this was because the petitioners themselves could not agree or could not raise the money, or because Elizabeth could not bear to think of permitting so many good men to leave her home kingdom. The latter seems much the more likely. The petitioners testified that they already had the capital, and the scheme had been thoroughly worked out and agreed upon before the petitions were presented. On the other hand, Elizabeth always was reluctant to see valuable servants leave England, for whatever purpose; she seems to have been obsessed by a fear that all her dependable men would desert her, leaving her alone and helpless on her island; and she was particularly anxious to keep her good mariners very close to her own shores all the time.

Or it may be that Elizabeth was afraid that Spain

would be angry—as Spain assuredly would be. If this suggestion seems unchivalrous, it is because the popular misconception of Elizabeth as a lion-hearted Queen, courageously defying the base Spaniards, persists in spite of all the evidence of history. She *did* defy the Spaniards toward the end of her reign; but in earlier times she quite obviously, and quite understandably, feared them; and the attitude of defiance finally adopted was forced upon her by circumstances and by a line of brilliant, distinguished courtiers and statesmen, of whom Humphrey Gilbert was one of the first and one of the most influential, who based their whole foreign policy on attacking Spain before Spain had a chance to attack England.

Or it may be that Elizabeth did not believe that the "gentlemen of the West Country" really intended to plant a colony anywhere at all. Early in her reign, while Humphrey Gilbert had been fighting at Havre de Grace, the Queen had suffered an unfortunate experience with a so-called colonizer. Thomas ("Lusty") Stukeley, another West Countryman, a distant relative of Humphrey Gilbert, had swaggered into her presence then and announced himself ready, if she would grant permission, to equip a fleet and sail to Florida, there to plant a colony, make it into a kingdom, and write to Elizabeth as "dear sister." How it happened that Elizabeth was taken in by this bombastical nonsense we do not know. But she permitted "Lusty" Stukeley to fit out his fleet; after which he did what anybody who had known the man must have expected him to do—he sold out to Philip of Spain and, making one of the many obscure little harbors of Ireland his base, became, instead of the mere dabbler in piracy he had been previously, a full-fledged sea bandit who preyed upon English shipping.

Elizabeth had made a sad mistake in that case, and

it may be that the experience had rendered her overcautious in dealing with would-be colonizers.

It is significant that, under the circumstances, the West Country gentlemen asked formal permission to undertake this venture they had planned. It became the custom, a little later, to go ahead and do the deed, and tell the Queen about it afterward. If it failed, you were a pirate and were hanged; but if it succeeded, you were a hero—and a millionaire to boot. Francis Drake worked on this principle, and he was sensationally successful. But some of these petitioning West Country gentlemen had tried it once, in Ireland, and had failed badly: they were not likely to burn their fingers twice in the same fire. Besides, I think we are safe in assuming that Humphrey Gilbert would not have been associated with any sort of enterprise which did not have the expressed approval of Elizabeth herself. For the man was, after all, every inch a courtier, implicitly a believer in the divine right of kings, and of queens. He never tried to go over Elizabeth's head; he never tried to go around her. Always, when he wanted a thing from her, he asked her directly, and if she refused it, he abided by her decision; for he was convinced that she could not be wrong. He never attempted, as sometimes other men did, to deceive her, trusting to revive her smiles later by enormous bribes. He never attempted to bring pressure to bear upon her to cause her to change her mind. To him, she was right; she was always right; she never could be anything *but* right.

CHAPTER XIII

A CELEBRATED ARGUMENT

MARTIN FROBISHER, that hulking Yorkshire man, seemed at last on the brink of promoting a voyage in search of the north-west passage Humphrey Gilbert had interested him in, in Ireland. Gilbert himself was not in the least jealous; on the contrary, he was generous with advice and invested a considerable sum of money, for him, in Frobisher's first voyage. It was Gilbert, too, who first set about obtaining for Frobisher the all-important influence at Court; he had introduced the seaman to Sir Henry Sidney, and through Sidney Frobisher met Sidney's brother-in-law, the Earl of Warwick, who was helping him immeasurably in money and influence. The Merchant Adventurers, true to form, bitterly opposed the proposal Frobisher advanced, but, thanks largely to Warwick's patronage, Frobisher was able to push them aside and proceed with his plans.

It has been said that Frobisher's voyages were made possible by the excitement created when Humphrey Gilbert's *Discourse of the Northwest Passage* first was published. This cannot be true, since the publication occurred several months after Frobisher had sailed, and many more months must be allowed for his preparations.

There can be no doubt, however, that the *Discourse*, and its author, were Frobisher's original inspiration. The celebrated *Discourse* was published, without Gilbert's permission—he had never intended it for publication—in 1576. But it had been passed about in manuscript form for ten years before that time, and it is impossible to believe that Martin Frobisher had not read it and pondered upon it.

Publication of the *Discourse* was brought about by another of Gilbert's eccentric friends—another pioneer, but a literary one—George Gascoigne.

This Gascoigne was a fascinating rogue who barely escaped being immortal. Born in 1537, two years before Humphrey Gilbert, he was the son of Sir John Gascoigne of Bedfordshire. He studied in Cambridge and was a member at Gray's Inn. He fought twice in the Low Countries, the second time under Humphrey Gilbert. About this second campaign he wrote a long and flamboyant poem, which, however, is a poor authority for a Gilbertian biography, being chiefly concerned with the personal (and not always laudable) adventures of of the poet himself.

Later this wag became a sort of hanger-on about the glittering Earl of Leicester, who lived in state like a royal personage. It was he who wrote the masques, songs, addresses, and entertainment for the elaborate celebration which attended Queen Elizabeth's visit to Leicester's castle of Kenilworth—an occasion made immortal by Sir Walter Scott. He was no classical pedant, like most of the literary men of the time, but a wholehearted disciple of Chaucer and Gower. His pioneering was extensive. He wrote the first prose comedy in English, the first English satire in regular verse, the first English short prose tales, the first English literary animadversion; and he was the first man to translate a tragedy into the English language. He was one of the earliest of the Mermaid Tavern goodfellows, and he had a genius for getting into trouble.

This amiable scallawag, then, early in 1576, was poking around in Humphrey Gilbert's library, and he asked Gilbert for a loan of the manuscript of the *Discourse*. Gilbert lent it cheerfully enough; and Gascoigne, after writing an introduction freely admitting that the deed was being done without Sir Humphrey's knowledge or permission, gaily published the thing.

It created a sensation; and it is, indeed, a most extraordinary document, even today. In spite of its many inaccuracies, it shows a stupendous erudition and a consuming desire for the truth. Originally designed to win the consent and possibly the financial backing of an older brother, it probably also was intended as a full statement on paper of the case for the north-west passage, and as such was meant for perusal by the doubting Thomases of the Merchant Adventurers.

There is no such thing as a passage between England and the Orient, by the north; but from the grand elevation of our present knowledge, it is all too easy to cast sneers upon the man who first insisted that there was. But though Gilbert, most of his lifetime, was practically alone in his belief, a voice crying in a wilderness, in time he did succeed in communicating that belief to his fellow countrymen, who with their native stubbornness held on to it for many years, for centuries. The *Discourse*, for all its errors, directly or indirectly inspired such discoverers and explorers as Frobisher, Raleigh, Davis, Waymouth, Hall, Knight, Hudson, Button, Gibbons, Bylot, Baffin, Hawkridge, Fox, James—to name only the earlier ones. Not until 1851, when Collinson and McClure definitely established the fact that no practicable passage existed, was the search for it abandoned; and meanwhile hundreds of lives had been lost and millions of pounds had been spent in the chasing of Sir Humphrey's mammoth will-o'-the-wisp. He may have been mistaken, but, characteristically enough, he was mistaken on a grand scale. Not until 1905 did a man actually sail from ocean to ocean north around North America: he was Roald Amundsen, in the tiny Norwegian *Gjoa*.

The *Discourse* runs to about 10,000 words, and comprises ten chapters. The first chapter cites classical authorities concerning Atlantis and the Americas—Plato, Marinæus Siculus, Marsilius Ficinus the Florentine, Crantor the Greek, Proclus, Philo the Jew, Aristotle, Strabo—and in addition quotes such modern geographers as Gemma Frisius, Muenster, Appianus, Franciscus Demongenitus, Peter Martyr, Ortelius, Hunter, Gastaldus, Guyccardinus, Michael Tramasinus, Bernard Puteanus, Andreas Vauasor, and Tramontanus. It also refers to an obscure narrative about a voyage made by Ochther in the time of King Alfred of Westsaxe, about 871 A.D., written in Saxon and translated into English by one M. Nowel, a servant of Lord Burghley.

"All which learned men and painful travellers have affirmed, with one consent and voice, that America was an Island: and that there lyeth a great Sea between it, Cataia, and Grondland [Greenland], by the which any man of our country, that will give the attempt, may with small danger pass to Cataia, the Moluccea, India, and all other places in the East, in much shorter time, than either the Spaniard, or Portugal doeth, or may do, from the nearest part of any of their countries within Europe."

He admits: "What moved these learned men to affirm thus much, I know not, or to what end so many and sundry travellers of both ages have allowed the same." But he adds: "But I conjecture that they would never have so constantly affirmed, or notified their opinions therein to the world, if they had not great good cause, and many probable reasons, to have led them thereunto."

Chapter Two points out that the streams of northeastern America get shallower near their mouths, but the further they are followed the deeper they become. If America were not an island, Gilbert argues here, then the Tartars and Scythians would have moved to it and the red Indians would have entered Asia. Paulus Venetus and Coronado never discovered or heard of a land passage from America to Asia, he writes, though they had penetrated deeper into America than any other travellers. Ocean currents must have *some* place to go, and some place to come from; and Jacques Cartier is quoted concerning the Labrador current, and Anthony Jenkinson concerning the current around the north of Russia.

Travellers who affirm that America is an island, Chapter Three states, include Venetus, Coronado, John Barros, de Gomara, Aluarus Nunnius, Cartier, Hieronymus Fracastorius the Italian, and finally England's own beloved Sebastian Cabot.

In Chapter Four it is set forth that the ancients told of red Indians tossed by a tempest on the coast of Germany. Pliny is quoted concerning Cornelius Nepos in connection with this tale. Red Indians were thrown upon the German coast again about the year 1160, in Frederick Barbarossa's time, and there are Gothic legends about them, the *Discourse* avers.

These Indians could not have come by the Cape of Good Hope ("Cape de buona Speranuca") or by the Magellan Straits, the fifth chapter declares—though it neglects to say *why* they couldn't.

Those Indians could not have come from the northeast because there was no navigable passage there; and even if there had been such a passage, they could not have negotiated it because of the cold and other difficulties.

Therefore (Chapter Seven) they must have come from the north-west. A Portuguese, a Dane, and a Spaniard, who made part of such a trip, also are vaguely mentioned in this chapter; and some additional classics are cited.

The eighth chapter contains Humphrey Gilbert's own account of a discussion he had with Anthony Jenkinson, leading proponent of the north-east passage, before the Queen and "certain lords of the Council." We have only Gilbert's word for this discussion; and naturally he does not make himself out to be on the losing side. When the discussion took place, we do not know. Very likely it was just after Sir Humphrey had presented his original petition for permission to seek a north-west passage, while he was back in England on leave from Ireland for the first time. He was in his middle twenties then, and Jenkinson was a seasoned seaman and scholar. Moreover, Jenkinson represented the powerful interests of the Merchant Adventurers, which opposed Gilbert's petition.

Jenkinson said he believed in the existence of a north-east passage. He had heard a Tartar fisherman say that he had once "sailed very far toward the Southeast, finding no end of the sea." Humphrey Gilbert answered this with the reminder that the Tartars were barbarians totally ignorant of the art of navigation and of geography, who wouldn't know south-east from north-east.

But Jenkinson had heard of an unicorn's horn being picked up on the Tartary coast, and there were no unicorns in Tartary: everybody knew that. Humphrey Gilbert replied that it was true enough that there were no unicorns in Tartary, and admitted that unicorns' horns don't "swimme"; but he said that he didn't think the barbarous "Tartarians" would know a real unicorn's horn if they saw one; it was possible that the tides might have carried this one back and forth, even though it couldn't "swimme"; anyway, it might have been the horn of the *Asinus Indicus*, which is plentiful in "Lappia, Norvegia, Finmarke, etc., as Jacobus Zieglerus writeth in his history of Scondia"; and besides all that, Albertus avers that there is a fish with one horn; "and therefore," concluded the triumphant young man, "it seemeth very doubtful both from whence it came, and whether it were an Unicorn's horn, yea, or no."

Jenkinson related that there is a continuous western current north of Russia. But Humphrey Gilbert replied that this meant nothing, and cited many similar currents, asserting that streams and freshets accounted for this flow of water.

So much for Mr. Jenkinson. But Chapter Nine declares that even if there *were* an eastern passage, the western passage would be better for English purposes because it was shorter, calmer, further south, and easier to fortify and control. Reference is made to Sir Hugh Willoughby, who with his crew was frozen in the ice all the winter of 1554-55 much farther south than the northernmost point it would be necessary to reach in order to sail north around America. Besides, the writer adds, the Muscovites would be sure to demand their share of any trading carried on around the north of Russia; whereas navigation of the north-*west* passage would not infringe upon the rights of any prince and would be entirely free.

And finally Chapter Ten contains a pretty picture of all the spoils in velvets, gold, silver, silks, cloth-of-gold, "or such like," and the advantages the system would have in developing a bigger and better navy, and in colonizing remote places with English paupers and criminals. The writer confesses his own lack of experience in travelling the seas to which he refers, but reminds the reader that he had "both the report, relations, and authority of divers most credible men, which have both seen and passed through some and every part of this discovery, besides sundry reasons for my assurance thereof: all which Columbus wanted."

The *Discourse* ends on a noble note, characteristic of Gilbertian writings:

"And therefore to give me leave without offence, always to live and die in this mind. He is not worthy to live at all, that for fear, or danger of death, shunneth his country's service, and his own honour: seeing death is inevitable, and the fame of virtue immortal. Wherefore in this behalf, *Multare vel timere sperno.*"

CHAPTER XIV

ALWAYS THE PIONEER

THE *Discourse* is the best known of Humphrey Gilbert's writings, and the only one which saw publication in his lifetime. He did not think of himself as a man of literature; he did not write for the sake of writing; always, when he took his pen, it was with some serious purpose in mind.

The *Discourse*, with its references to obscure classical writers and unicorns' horns and all the rest of it, today seems quaint, and unquestionably it is obsolete, useful to us only because it gives us a picture of the time and an insight into the character and beliefs of the author. *Queen Elizabeth's Achademy*, another discourse which he wrote about this time, is quite different. Less celebrated than the geographical essay, it contains many a meaty lesson which could well be pondered by any living person interested in education; and indeed, it has been quoted recently by some educational authorities. It constitutes (as if such a thing were needed!) another crushing refutation of the charge sometimes carelessly made that Humphrey Gilbert was, really, little more than a glorified pirate, a bloodthirsty captain with a smattering of knowledge, an aristocratic roughneck like so many of his picturesque but perhaps deplorable relatives.

Gentle Humphrey Gilbert is concerned, in this discourse, not with educating the common people—he never bothered about *them!*—but rather with bettering the minds, bodies, and morals of those members of the upper classes who for better or for worse governed

England in his time. He attacks the loose, vicious system of education which had been in operation for centuries: this was a system which had been repeatedly assailed from high places, but which survived largely because nobody came forward to suggest a better one.

Sons and daughters of knights and gentlemen were placed in great households, where they were obliged to wait on the lord's table and perform other menial offices, in return for which they were supposed to be trained in the gentle arts and in learning. Generally they were known as wards. In the royal household they were called, originally, henxmen, and later henchmen—which latter word had a quite different meaning from its present one. The Lord Chancellor of England was also Master of Wards for the royal household; and with lesser personages, dukes and earls and the like, he was charged with supervising the practical education of young England, especially of the men who would soon be governing that nation. These wards were to be taught not to spit on the table at meals, not to dip their meat into salt cellars, not to talk with their mouths full, not to pick their teeth. . . .[1] They were also to be taught some little book learning, and rather more of physical and martial exercises.

The results were deplorable. The lords frequently farmed out their wards, finding them a nuisance; and the substitute instructors more often than not were ignorant men concerned only with spending as little money as possible on the wards and splitting the fees with the higher-ups originally charged with the educational task.

Sometimes, too, the system was twisted to serve political ends. A lord took in many more wards than he could possibly give real attention to, knowing that the chances were that these young men, when they took

---

[1] This is not meant to be funny. These "don'ts," and many similar ones, actually were recommended to ward farmers for their charges.

their places in Court later, would remain members of his following through either sentimentality or sheer habit.

Sir Nicholas Bacon, father of Francis Bacon, was Master of Wards in the early part of Elizabeth's reign. On his resignation he offered many recommendations for the alteration of the system. They were good recommendations, but they went unheeded. Wrote Sir Nicholas: "Hitherto the chief care of governance hath been to the land, being the meanest; and to the body, being the better, very small; but the mind, being the best, none at all; which methinks is plainly to set the cart before the horse."

Now Burghley was Master of Wards; and learned men continued to attack the system in vain. The same year that Sir Nicholas resigned, 1561, Sir Thomas Hobey published *The Courtier*, his translation from the Italian of Baldassare Castiglioni's excellent *Cortigiano*. It told what the true courtier ought to be, and—in England, at least—usually wasn't.

In 1570 that sweet-tempered pedagogue, Roger Ascham, who had helped to supervise the education of the Princess Elizabeth and also, probably, that of her page, Humphrey Gilbert, published *The Scholemaster*, a model for educators of all times. He asked for much greater stress on book learning and much less on physical exercises, bewailing the fact that "commonly the young gentlemen of England go unwillingly to school, but run to the stable." From what we can learn of them, the stable was just where most of them belonged. But the fact remained that they were the men who would have England's destiny in their hands very soon. Roger Ascham and Baldassare Castiglioni, commendable as their works are, offered no practical, immediate solution to what they admitted was a serious problem.

Not so Humphrey Gilbert. Here was a man who, for

all his dreaming, strove always to be practical. And he was perfectly fitted to suggest changes in the ward system; for he was an all-around man, at once a bookworm and a first-class butcher, a learned linguist and a cool captain in battle, who could and did both dream and do.

In *Queen Elizabeth's Achademy*, written only as a paper for Her Majesty's private perusal, he found the current system in all respects deplorable. The wards were, "for the most part brought up in idleness and lascivious pastimes, estranged from all servacable virtues." All too often the farmers not only failed to educate their wards, but deliberately worked to prevent them from getting any real education, for fear that they might become too good, too self-respecting, to be inveigled into marrying the daughters of these farmers and so bring money into the miserable family—so Humphrey Gilbert declared.

Specifically, what he proposed was the establishment by the Queen of a large academy in London, where all gentlemen's sons would be educated, so that "there shall be hereafter no gentleman within this realm but is good for something; whereas now, the most part of them are good for nothing."

He complained that Cambridge and Oxford taught only book learning. He desired to teach much more than that. The essential purpose behind his plan was the service of the state; and he was very earnest about it.

He had the whole thing worked out. He thought of everything.

There should be a classical-language professor, with two ushers to assist him. There should also be a professor of Hebrew.

There should be a professor of logic and rhetoric; and the author lays considerable emphasis upon the need

ALWAYS THE PIONEER

for a good knowledge of one's own language, "the choice of words, the building of sentences, the garnishment of figures, and other beauties of Oratory."

To the teacher of moral philosophy should be assigned the duty of imparting to the students a knowledge of civil and martial politics. Chaucer is quoted here to the effect that "the greatest school clerks are not always the wisest men."

There should be (of course!) a lecturer on divinity.

The mathematics professor should be instructed to pay particular attention to the art of navigation, knowledge of the stars and constellations, and the use of nautical instruments. A model of a full-rigged ship should be provided in his classroom for demonstration purposes.

There should be a professor of geometry, too, and part of his duty should be the teaching of the theory and practice of artillery. For Humphrey Gilbert was not one of those military men who advocated the scrapping of all firearms and a general return to the longbow.

In addition, there should be an experienced soldier, a war veteran, who could teach the students "to ride, make ready and handle a horse," and instruct them in all other martial exercises.

There should be a doctor of physic, and his duties would be numerous and important. He should teach first aid—though it wasn't called that then; the practice and theory of chemistry, being specifically admonished to use plain language;[1] the use of all common simples and cures; and, unexpectedly, surgery.

[1] The experience with William Meadley had not shaken Sir Humphrey's faith in the transmutation of metals—a faith he shared with practically every other man of his time. There was on the statute-books an old law forbidding the transmutation of lead or iron coins into gold coins; and the author of *Queen Elizabeth's Achademy* was careful to provide that his doctor of physic, if any of his experiments along these lines proved successful, should be specifically exempt from prosecution under this law.

Here Sir Humphrey literally was centuries ahead of his time. This is probably the first serious proposal, certainly the first in the English language, that medicine and surgery be united. The author explains that his reason for suggesting this radical step is the fact that "Chirugerie [surgery] is not now to be learned in any other place than a Barber's shop, and in that shop most dangerous especially in time of plague, when the ordinary trimming of men for cleanliness must be done by those which have to do with infected persons." He had not forgotten the men who died all around him at Havre de Grace.

There should be a lecturer on civil law, and also a practising lawyer, "it being most necessary that noblemen and gentlemen should learn to be able to put their own cases in law, and to have some judgement in the office of a Justice of Peace and Sheriff."

Then there should be separate instructors for French, Spanish, Italian, and High Dutch, this making a total of eight languages to be taught, including English.

Finally there should be men who would teach "dauncing, vawting, and musick," for these, too, were accomplishments of every properly trained gentleman. And there should be an expert on heraldry.

The whole business was worked out to the smallest detail, and it contains many suggestions which astound the reader with their modernity. For example, it was provided that in addition to their regular work of instruction, the members of the faculty of Queen Elizabeth Academy should be required to write and issue a series of publications, at stated intervals, embodying the results of their studies and experiments. Precisely this system is used in many great universities today.

The library which would be a requisite for such an institution is by no means forgotten. Sir Humphrey would have had a law that "all printers in England for ever should be charged to deliver to the Library of the Academy, at their own charges, one copy, well bound, of every book, proclamation, or pamphlet that they shall print." This anticipated by centuries the laws which created the British Museum library, the greatest collection of books in the world today, and the United States Library of Congress.

This entire institution, Sir Humphrey calculates with appalling nicety, could be conducted as outlined on an annual appropriation of £2,966, 13 shillings, and 4 pence.

But the man was foredoomed to be a failure in everything he undertook. The tragedy of his life was utter, complete. A cat's-paw in France, he had done his best to keep Havre de Grace for the English; and politics and the plague had taken Havre de Grace away. Relentless, single-purposed, highly efficient as an Irish governor, he had subdued Munster, according to his orders —but the moment he had turned his back all Munster was in arms again; and the question he had honestly endeavored to answer for all time, by means of fire and sword, lingered for centuries to perplex his countrymen. All his grand projects for conquering remote parts of the New World for England were laughed at, turned aside, or ignored; all the hours, the weeks, and years he had spent in studying the art of navigation and the science of geography seemed only wasted. Once more a political scapegoat, he had been sent on a hopeless and thankless errand to the Low Countries; the fighting he had done there had kept the Spaniards busy for a time and helped to give the Prince of Orange an opportunity to assemble and train his men for a final decisive campaign, so that in the long run Gilbert's part in assisting to found the Republic of the United Netherlands, in 1609, was much more important than appears at a glance; but he returned to England in disgrace, with a record of battles lost and sieges broken.

And now—not a crack-brained Quixote, but a brilliant-minded, well-trained, sincere, and high-purposed student and man of the world—he had ventured to break a lance with the incalculably vast forces of evil and darkness and greed and ignorance which were keeping his nation from fulfilling her appointed destiny. Single-handed he had galloped at them.

Of course it was another failure. Indeed, it was a failure so profound that it seems to have left no immediate echo. Perhaps Queen Elizabeth read the *Achademy* through, and perhaps she didn't. If she did, she put it aside, shuddering, when she learned that this astounding innovation would cost her £2,966, 13s. and 4d. a year. Why, it cost her nothing at all, under the current system, to have the wards trained! It may be that they weren't *well* trained; that was quite possible. But Elizabeth, herself a highly educated woman, never took the slightest interest in the education of her subjects.

Probably it did not even occur to courtier Gilbert to do anything further about his proposed academy. He was no agitator; he was no professional reformer. He had not sought to present this plan to the world at large, or even to the English people; he merely had sought to present it to the Queen. And when the Queen refused to act upon it, that was the end of the matter—and this discourse, so patriotic, so well thought out, so profoundly foresighted, was put aside to gather dust, neglected until comparatively recently, when somebody discovered it, a museum item, in one of the very institutions it had anticipated.

CHAPTER XV

FROBISHER AMONG THE ESKIMOS

HIS work, now, was bearing at least a little fruit. The Merchant Adventurers, slowly enough, but surely, were turning to his way of thinking. More than ever it was becoming clear that England, in sheer self-defence, must find some new trade route to the Orient. To be sure, Elizabeth's thriftiness—to give it a polite name—was producing results. Open war was being avoided, at whatever cost. The Queen's "frenzied grasp on her money bags," often dangerous and always disgusting, *was* helping to raise England's credit in the world of finance; the government was borrowing money in Antwerp at only 5 per cent, though Elizabeth's predecessors had been obliged to pay 14 per cent. But the fact remained that the Spaniards and Portuguese, and notably the Spaniards, were getting all the gold, and that England, without some substantial resources not visible within her own boundaries, never would be able to compete with the Peninsular nations.

Gold was what was needed. Gold! more gold! Everybody desired it; everybody talked about it. From the throne down, it glittered pauselessly in English dreams.

Humphrey Gilbert, too, required money.

Walter Raleigh was working with him and for him now. Brother Walter was a straight, sharp-eyed young man, ambitious, arrogant, efficient, utterly loyal to his half-brother. He had fought for the Huguenots in France, and now he was back in London, handsome and obscure, a daredevil, ready for anything. They worked well together, these two. There was a difference of fourteen years in their ages, but they worked together, dreamed together, consulted, read, argued with mutual enemies and mutual friends. "My true brother," Walter Raleigh called Sir Humphrey.

At the moment, however, Walter Raleigh's assistance was necessarily moral rather than material. Sir Humphrey did not have much money, but brother Walter did not have *any*. Sir Humphrey's influence at Court was not sufficient for his purposes; but brother Walter, as far as the Queen was concerned, was an insignificant hanger-on, a nobody; it is possible that she had never even set eyes on him at this time.

The most terrible and most wonderful thing about this age in England, for the men who lived it, was the fact that nobody ever knew what the Queen was going to do next. Very likely she herself never knew. When she did make some decision, she changed her mind the next moment—and then changed it again—and changed it yet again—until her servants were wild with anxiety and exasperation.

Possibly the woman was not wholly sane. The circumstance that she had a keen mind, a nimble tongue, a perfect sense of politics, means little—at least, it does not in itself argue sanity.

Certainly, at any rate, she was quite a different woman from the gentle-spoken, so very humble princess Humphrey Gilbert had attended as a page. She had been on the throne for two decades, and how they had changed her! Her greed, her unreliability, her utter inconsistency, have been mentioned. Her appearance, too, had altered. Outwardly the scornful, upright monarch, privately she was enduring tortures. Attended by physicians incredibly incompetent, to whom she paid little attention anyway, she had at this time already been a victim of jaundice, chicken pox, smallpox, whooping-cough, dropsy, anæmia, recurring fevers, neuralgia, chronic gastro-intestinal disorders. . . . Her hair had fallen out and she had taken to wearing wigs—dozens of different wigs, most of them red. Her teeth, after giving her untold pain, had mostly fallen out or been extracted, and those that remained had turned black. She was subject to headaches and fainting-spells. She caught cold easily. She never slept well. She suffered from a horrible ulcer in her leg, which quite possibly—modern physicians cannot say for certain—was a symptom of syphilis inherited from that reprobate, Henry VIII.

Small wonder, then, that the sweet-tempered, careful princess had become an irascible, ranting, cursing Queen, given to unexpected fits of loud and shocking gaiety, altogether unpredictable, and quite possibly mad.

Yet she was an absolute monarch, the last that England was to know. Nothing could be done without her permission. Nothing that she commanded, however dishonourable, however difficult or distasteful, could be left undone—or at least unattempted.

She, and not the faulty sea cards, the current ignorance of geography, the waves, fogs, icebergs—not even the difficulty of raising capital—she, the Queen, was the biggest obstacle in Humphrey Gilbert's path. There was no way to sidestep her; she *would* not be denied; she must be surmounted.

Not long after Elizabeth had failed to sanction the southern colonization plan, Martin Frobisher, working through a different channel of Court influence, obtained his long-sought permission to seek a north-west passage. He made three voyages, in 1576, 1577, and 1578; and because Humphrey Gilbert was largely the original inspiration for these voyages, because he was actively interested in them, both as a man of business and as a student of geography and navigation, and because their results affected so profoundly his own chances of setting sail for the land of his dreams—because of these things it is worth while to summarize the Frobisher voyages here.

The Yorkshire man was thirty-eight years old when he started the first voyage—large, blond, quiet, a stern commander, almost illiterate. Certainly an ex-slaver, probably an ex-pirate, his past was shady. But he inspired confidence where Humphrey Gilbert, perhaps, did not. True, he did not possess one-twentieth of Gilbert's book knowledge of navigation; but then, as Frobisher's biographer, himself a practical seaman,[1] points out: "The gift of being a good navigator . . . is no respecter of persons. That it is a gift, and a science, is generally admitted. It also happens to be an art. The finest equipment known to man will never change a bad navigator into a good one. And the born navigator, on the other hand, such as Frobisher was, rises supreme above the most contemptible craft to which he may be appointed."

Very quietly, then, this master mariner who didn't know much about books sailed with three ships that were most emphatically "contemptible." This was in June, 1576. The 7-ton pinnace was lost. The 25-ton *Michael* turned back when her commander lost his nerve, deserting. But Frobisher's flagship, the *Gabriel*, 20 tons, struggled along until, on July 26th, Resolution Island, off Baffin Land, was sighted.[2]

Frobisher traded briefly, and cautiously, with some Eskimos—treacherous fellows. He poked about, here and there, unable to locate the north-west passage he had come to seek, but seeing many things certain to impress the folks back home. He lost five of his men,

---

[1] *The Life of Sir Martin Frobisher,* by William McFee.

[2] But they didn't know it was an island, then. They named it Queen's Foreland.

in the only lifeboat the *Gabriel* carried, when they disobeyed his command and went ashore for further trading. He took as souveniers some samples of the all-too-scant vegetation, some pieces of stone and rock—and notably one large black stone—and an Eskimo.

This Eskimo, paddling his kayak, had ventured too close to the *Gabriel*, the deck of which was only a few feet above the water. Burly Frobisher leaned over the rail, and, grabbing the fellow, hoisted him, kayak and all, to the deck. They took him back to England, where naturally he attracted much attention, and where he caught cold and died.

All this was interesting, but not lucrative. The voyage had added little to current geographical knowledge; it had contributed nothing toward the belief that there was a north-west passage to India; and, more immediately, it had cost its backers, among them Sir Humphrey Gilbert, a lot of good money. Frobisher remained obscure, more or less discredited, with an £800 deficit and no prospect of raising capital for the second voyage he desired to make.

That winter of 1576-77, the principal financier of the enterprise, Michael Lock, decided to have the black stone examined by metallurgists, to be certain that it didn't contain gold. Three experts examined it and reported it to be iron pyrites, or marascite, virtually worthless. A fourth assayist—an Italian, and probably also a rascal—muttered mysteriously *"bisogna sapere adulare la nature"*—"sometimes nature needs a little coaxing"—and produced a tiny pile of gold dust he said he had extracted from the black stone. A second foreigner backed this finding.

Immediately there was vast excitement in England. *Gold!* What madness that word could inspire! For his first voyage Frobisher had experienced the greatest difficulty raising capital, but now he was swamped by would-be investors. The Queen herself, who had shown not the slightest interest in the original trip, now suddenly became much concerned about the second; and she contributed a big ship, £1,000, and many encouraging words, and began to dictate how many men should go, in how many ships, and what they should do and how they should do it. The Company of Cathay was organized in March, 1577; the original deficit was gladly paid off, and a few months later Frobisher again set sail for the New World. He had become, abruptly, a very important man indeed.

The fleet this time consisted of the *Gabriel*, the *Michael*, and the Queen's ship, the *Aid*, a 200-tonner, which loomed above her sisters like a modern liner above the tugs that push and fuss her into dock. The *Aid* was to be filled with this black stone and then was to be sent back to England without delay. After that, Frobisher could do what he liked and go where he liked with his own ships. Elizabeth was not at all anxious about the north-west passage, but she was very anxious indeed about the black stone.

Frobisher explored much the same district as he had explored on his first voyage; named sundry bays, islands, and mountains after influential friends at Court; tried to capture another Eskimo and succeeded only in getting an arrow in a most unsoldierly place, and ran away, bellowing, his hands over his buttocks; later did manage to grab one of those pesky natives; and finally loaded the *Aid* with several hundred tons of iron pyrites, according to orders, and sailed back to England.

That summer was finished—and the seas Frobisher sailed were navigable only for a few months of each year. There was much excitement about the black stones, which were transferred, under heavy guard, to the Tower of London and to Portland Castle, where they were placed in vaults quadruply locked. And without delay, plans for a third voyage were launched. Again Frobisher found no difficulty getting money; the Queen was more thrilled than ever, and the third voyage, unlike the second, was to be not merely semi-official, but under the direct supervision of the Crown.

Of greater interest to us today—and probably of greater interest to Humphrey Gilbert at the time—was the fact that this third voyage was going to endeavor to plant the first English colony in the New World.

This colony was not to care for a nation's overflow, or give a persecuted religious group a place to worship in peace, or glorify the name of England by extending England's boundaries. It was to be purely and simply a mining camp, a winter camp, where the black stone would be torn from the bowels of the earth in readiness for the coming of more ships, the following summer, to take it away. In short, it was to be something similar to the colony Humphrey Gilbert himself had first proposed. *He* had desired a semi-permanent settlement to act as a sort of base of supplies, a haven, for Englishmen making the north-west passage. This dream had since grown, as Humphrey Gilbert's dreams were wont to grow, until it envisaged the establishment of a permanent empire over the seas. But originally the colonization dream had been much like this plan of Frobisher's; and it is quite possible that Humphrey Gilbert had something to do with this feature of the plan for Frobisher's third voyage. It is certain, at least, that Frobisher consulted with Gilbert, and that Gilbert was intensely interested in the Frobisher ventures—as interested, probably, as any person in England, even Elizabeth.

There were fifteen ships this time. Twelve of them, including the two the Queen was contributing, were to return in the fall, laden with black stones. The other three were to remain at Resolution Island, where the colony was to be established. The colonists were to be thirty Cornish miners, thirty soldiers, and forty sailors to man the three ships.

The first English habitation it was proposed to build in the New World was to be a ready-made affair, a sort of portable fort with living-quarters, constructed in the mother country and transported in sections in three of the ships. Carpenters, on these ships, were to assemble the building.

And now, in his prosperity, in the heyday of his fame, stout Martin Frobisher found himself having troubles he had always managed to avoid when he was an obscure and penniless mariner. The seas battered the ships without mercy. Icebergs were always about. The fogs remained with them for days, even for weeks, so that it was not always possible for them to keep together. One of them, the 100-ton *Dennis*, was rammed by an iceberg and went to the bottom; all hands were rescued, but the *Dennis* had carried the north and west sides of the proposed fort, and these were lost.

Frobisher, as admiral, was in supreme command; but he was unaccustomed to the handling of big fleets; and the fifteen ships' masters, he soon learned, had fifteen different ideas about the way things should be done. Frobisher didn't listen very politely.

In the fog and general confusion, they somehow sailed for a long distance up what we know now was the present Hudson Straits; but at first, they supposed them to be the original discovery, Frobisher's Straits. They learned their mistake and turned back, and in time did find Frobisher's Straits again; but meanwhile the admiral was wondering whether he hadn't stumbled upon that north-west passage Humphrey Gilbert was forever talking about. However, he had no authority to seek any farther for it. He was sent out for black rock, and nothing else but black rock.

FROBISHER AMONG THE ESKIMOS 109

They had every sort of trouble conceivable. And at the end of the summer, it having been agreed that the establishment of a colony under the circumstances would be "very impossible," they returned to England. There they learned that the black stone at last had been found, indubitably, to be worthless; it had been cast out of the vaults in Portland Castle and the Tower of London, and was being used to pave roads. The persons who had been so very anxious to invest money in the enterprise, believing everything that was told them once the word "gold" had been spoken, now were highly indignant and demanded that this man and that man be punished. The Cathay Company went into the hands of a receiver. Michael Lock, married, penniless now, and the father of fifteen children, was thrown into jail without a trial. Frobisher, hooted and hissed, was a bankrupt; he kept out of jail, but no longer was he an admiral, and he was considered lucky to obtain command of a single ship under Sir William Winter, in Ireland; he never made any further attempt to sail the northern seas, though he subsequently distinguished himself, and won a knighthood, in the fight against the Spanish Armada.[3]

[3] In 1862, almost three hundred years later, Captain C. F. Hall, U. S. N., landed on the place Frobisher had named Countess of Warwick Island, and he spent two years among the Eskimos in those parts. The Eskimos called the island Kodlunarn, or White Man's Island, and they told Hall that many years before white men had come there but had gone away again. Moreover, they showed the American—who at the time was unacquainted with the details of the Frobisher voyages—bricks, tiles, pieces of buried wood, and a "bloom" of iron no doubt left by one of Frobisher's metal-workers. Further, they told him the handed-down tale of what had happened to the five men Frobisher had lost on his first expedition. These men, it appears, had not been killed, as Frobisher had supposed. They had, in later years, found the lime and stone house the third expedition had erected (Captain Hall saw this house) and therein they had found trinkets, bells, and other articles the never-launched fourth expedition was to have used in trade with the natives. Near this house the five stranded Englishmen, according to Eskimo traditions, had found buried the surviving sections of that fort which never was assembled; and out of these

And so, through no fault of his, Humphrey Gilbert's dream once more had been discredited. No doubt he himself believed more firmly than ever in the existence of a north-west passage: the tale of the "Mistaken Strait," which went directly west and seemed to have no ending, assuredly would strengthen his faith, if that needed strengthening.

Meanwhile, however, this always-busy man was off at another tangent. Once again he was proposing a grandiose scheme for the glory of England and of his own pocketbook—a breathlessly audacious scheme to establish an empire beyond the seas. And now, for the first time, it really seemed as though he would be given a chance to prove his statements: it really looked as though he would be put to the one true test.

Here he was, forty years old, immeasurably ambitious, incalculably eager for adventure, yet ever since he had been a lad confined to what must have seemed to him a cage—forced to perform difficult but thankless tasks, obliged to fight in sneaky, dishonourable wars—dreaming, scheming, soaring in his imagination to the remotest corners of the earth, yet always kept by an eccentric monarch intolerably close to the hearthstone. Here he was; and at last it seemed that he was to be permitted to do something that he wanted to do. The cage was to be opened, the eagle freed.

---

timbers they had constructed a boat, in which they had sailed away for an England they never reached.

CHAPTER XVI

PIRACY, LTD.

SOME students have confessed themselves unable to distinguish between the notions of piracy and of patriotism prevalent in Elizabeth's time. Yet the distinction is clear enough and perfectly simple. A pirate who succeeded was a patriot, whereas a pirate who failed was simply a pirate. When Francis Bacon warned Sir Walter Raleigh that an action he proposed would be nothing less than piracy, the knight is said to have replied, scornfully, "Who ever heard of a man being a pirate for millions?" The story may not be true; but the sentiment it expressed was perfectly sound—in those times.

If you, my reader, having come this far in the story of Sir Humphrey Gilbert, have been picturing him in your mind as something of a saint, spattered perhaps by the mud of war and corrupt politics, but spattered rather as an innocent victim, and always in his heart of hearts motivated by the highest ideals of patriotism and service to humankind—if you have come to believe that he was utterly unselfish, a man above the scoundrels by whom he was surrounded, and not subject to their greed and baseness—then the fault has been mine, and this job, so far, misleading.

In fact, Humphrey Gilbert, like most of the other extraordinary men of Elizabeth's extraordinary Court, had at least his full share of avarice. True, there was much that was noble about the man; but there was also much that was low, despicable. Beyond question, his loyalty was amazing—his loyalty to his country, to his

Queen, to his family, and his friends. His gifts were great, and probably the greatest of these was that of serene faith. His industry was astounding. He had a brilliant mind, magnificent courage. But all this does not mean that there was not, behind most of the grand plans with which he pelted his sovereign, discernible always a good, big, sordid, commercial motive. Oh, he was not a hypocrite! He really intended to advance the welfare of his Queen and his country in everything he undertook. But he also intended, if possible, to make money. He had some money of his own, but not enough. His wife had a considerable fortune, but even that did not satisfy this impatient, this immensely restless man. What were hundreds of pounds, what were thousands, even, to one who desired millions uncountable? What was this little estate, that petty manor, to one who dreamed of being the ruler of at least half the world? Money—money was what was needed, first of all.

Humphrey Gilbert, in fact, was a typical Elizabethan just because he *was* such a mass of contradictions. Dreaming of Bambyce silk, and cloth-of-gold, and pepper and spices from far Oriental lands, he still could glory in slaughter like a homicidal maniac amuck with an axe. Exquisitely dressed, his beard trimmed and perfumed, rings in his ears, roses in his shoe latchets, he could sit in an arena with the other dandies of the Court, and watch dogs tear a chained bear into horrid, bloody pieces. He was not double-natured; he was *multiple*-natured. He was not good one day and bad the next; he was good and bad at one and the same time. He gave over all the resources of his keen mind to the task of trying to better the conditions of England's youth, producing the brilliant and wholly altruistic *Achademy*; and with, as it were, the same pen, and seated at the same writing-table, he planned and set forth on paper one of the coolest, most insolent schemes for systematic murder and piracy that ever the world has known.

For it must have been about the same time that he was working out the *Achademy* idea, that Sir Humphrey wrote still another discourse for his Queen—the breath-taking *How Her Majesty may annoy the King of Spain.*

The thing was submitted to Elizabeth November 6, 1577, and it survives today. It was surrounded by a great air of mystery; certain proper names contained in it are concealed, not very cleverly, by initials—thus, Newfoundland is "N.L.," the West Indies are the "W.I.," the Spaniards are "the S." It was signed, but the signature has been scratched out with another pen. That signature appears to be "H. Gylberte." This was the way he invariably spelt his own name, though others spelt it a multitude of different ways. The document is not in Humphrey Gilbert's handwriting, but it is emphatically in Gilbert's own literary style, and the ideas are decidedly his. A second discourse, which supplements it, and to which there is a reference in the first discourse, is not signed at all; but this again bears unmistakably the stamp of Gilbert's authorship.

"Annoy" is an amusing enough word, in view of what was proposed.

In the opening paragraph the writer formally prostrates himself before his monarch, protesting that he is but "a silly member of this Common weal of England, and do not offer myself therein as an Instructor, or as a reformer, but as a Wellwisher to your Majesty and my Country, wherein the meanest or simplest ought not to yield them selves second to the best, or wisest."

"And so," he continues, with unexpected crispness after the pomposity of that beginning —— "and so to the matter."

Wars are evils, he states—with no startling display

or originality, to be sure—but some wars are necessary, wars of defence. Now the best defence is attack. Hit your enemy before he has an opportunity to hit you: this is the creed that motivates the entire discourse. Strike first, and strike hard.

England, in order to defend herself against her enemies, must at the same time strengthen herself and weaken the said enemies. One thing is as important as the other. The civil wars of France and Philip's troubles are briefly referred to, but the writer hastens on, apologizing. "And for that this your Majesty's Realm of England requireth other considerations than those which are on the continent, I will omit them, and spin a thread proper for our English looms."

He admonishes the Queen always to walk in the ways of God, and warns her in the same paragraph that the "leagues and fair words" of foreign princes "ought to be held but as Mermaids' songs, sweet poisons . . . that abuse with outward plausibility, and gay shows." Also, he points out, solemnly: "Christian princes ought not for any respect to combine themselves in amity with such as are at open and professed war with god himself"—in other words, with Roman Catholics.

Then he advances his proposition. He would form a company—he is prepared to raise the capital: the Queen will not be asked for material coöperation—which would equip some ships and arm some men, and with these would go to the Grand Banks and there fall upon the Spanish, Portuguese, and French fishing-vessels. If the Queen thinks this too much at first, he is willing to confine himself to the Spanish and French vessels, or even just to the Spanish. But the Spanish certainly, in any event. This would be done unofficially, and ostensibly without the knowledge of the Queen—in short, another "underhand war," but a naval one. The pirates would assert that they were acting for the Prince of Orange, say, or some other open enemy of King Philip. And "after the public notice of which fact, your majesty is either to avow the same (if by the event thereof it shall so seem good) or to disavow both them and the fact, as league breakers; leaving them to pretend it was done without your privity, either in the service of the prince of Orange or otherwise."

"This cloak being had for the reign," then, the thing to do would be send the ships to "N.L."—"which with your good license I will undertake without your Majesty's charge"—and there they would pounce upon the all-unwarned fishing-vessels. "I would have take and bring away with their freights and ladings, the best of those ships and to burn the worst." What would happen to the crews is a matter upon which the writer, with rare delicacy, does not touch. The ships would be taken to Holland or Zeeland and the cargoes sold; or else, "under the friendship of some certain vice admiral of this realm; who may be afterwards committed to prison, as in displeasure of the same," they could be herded into one of the small bays on the coast of Ireland or England—all, of course, without the knowledge of the Queen. Six months' food and four months' drink should be provided at this hiding-place by the scapegoat admiral.

Meanwhile, and elsewhere in England, the war company would be quietly assembling a force of 5,000 or 6,000 men, with munitions, "which men with certain other ships of war being in a readiness, shall pretend to inhabit St. Lawrence Island [in Canada], the late discovered Countries in the North, or elsewhere; and not to join with the others; but in some certain remote place at sea."

Observe how ingeniously it is all worked out! Humphrey Gilbert had been petitioning Elizabeth for years to plant a colony on or near St. Lawrence Island; that this was his life passion was well known to everybody in official life, and assuredly to King Philip's spies; hence there would be nothing suspicious about this gathering of a second force under his leadership.

The proceeds of the first venture would defray the expenses of the second; already King Philip would have been well "annoyed"; and the two fleets, united at sea, were to descend upon the West Indies and deliberately snatch these from the Spaniards.

"It were better a thousand times thus to gain the starts of them," Humphrey Gilbert points out.

For assuredly, though Spain and England were at peace, Spain was merely waiting for her opportunity to attack England. He seems to have believed this absolutely: there is an unmistakable ring of honesty in the whole discourse. The writer admits that while Elizabeth might conceal from other princes her connection with the piracies, she could not conceal it from God, Who sees everything. But, he adds, "I hold it is lawful in christian policy, to prevent a mischief betimes: as to revenge it too late."

The writer coolly continues: "If your highness will permit me, with my associates, either overtly or covertly to perform the forsaid enterprise: then with the gain thereof there may easily be such a competent company transported to the W.I., as may be able not only to dispossess the S. thereof, but also to possess for ever your Majesty and Realm therewith."

He offers to explain in detail, if Elizabeth desires it, his already-mapped-out plan of campaign for capturing the West Indies.

"But," he finishes, knowing his monarch and her seemingly incurable propensity to vacillate and postpone, "if your Majesty like to do it at all, then would I wish your highness to consider that delay doth often times

TYPICAL FIGHTING-SHIP OF THE TIME

prevent the performance of good things: for the wings of mans life are plumed with the feathers of death."

This time the Queen was interested. *This* discourse held her attention. Evidently she asked to see the supplement, the promised outline for the West Indian campaign; for this document was presented soon afterward. It is entitled *A Discourse hoe hir Matie may meete with and annoy the K. of Spayne*, and it is about the same length as the original discourse.

It starts: "It is most certain and true that the king of Spain is wholly addicted to the Pope, and is the chief maintainer of the Romish religion . . . and thereby an enemy to all others that be not of the same religion."

Again the lesson is: strike first. "It is good cause to provide before hand how and by what means such and so great a prince as the king of Spain is, with all the whole troop of Catholics, may best be withstanded and most endamaged with least charges to the Queens Majesty . . . by what means the king of Spain may be brought to know that any kind of peace shall be better for him than wars with England."

Once more the pioneer—for this attitude, in fact, was precisely the one Elizabeth eventually was induced to take toward Spain.

Humphrey Gilbert would "withstand" Philip by pouncing first upon Cuba and the island of Hispaniola, now San Domingo. These two islands, he writes, were not well defended, not heavily garrisoned, and should fall easy victims to the English army he proposed to lead against them. The discourse is at some pains to point out that these islands provide plenty of food and provisions for a large force of Englishmen, and once taken could easily be defended. It adds, of course, something about their riches, the gold and silver mines, and the profitable trade that could be developed with the mother country.

Cuba and Hispaniola were the key islands of the whole West Indian territory, the writer states. Once they were captured, the rest would be easy; all Philip's enormous sources of wealth would be snipped off, and London and Plymouth soon would be receiving those shipments of riches that were now, alas, all going to Corunna, Cadiz, Seville.

There was an alternative plan submitted. And here again Gilbert was ahead of his time, for it was this second plan, as first suggested by him, that eventually became the naval policy of Elizabethan England toward Spain. It was, briefly, to lay in wait for the annual Spanish plate-fleet—the treasure-ships which carried Mexican gold and Peruvian silver to Philip's home country—to descend upon this fleet without warning, to sack it thoroughly, and to pocket the proceeds. For this purpose, Gilbert suggested making the islands of Bermuda a coign of vantage. Bermuda, he explained, was about fifty leagues from the Bahamas. After that fleet got out of the island district, got out into the open ocean, it might take any one of several courses back to Spain, and so might avoid the English fleet that was waiting to surprise it; whereas, before it got to the Bahamas, it would not be fully loaded with riches; hence, clearly, the Bahamas was the place to catch it.

Now, what did Elizabeth think of this little scheme?

Apparently Elizabeth thought very well of it. She couldn't publicly endorse it, of course, but it was a plan after her own heart. She accepted no responsibility; she could not be forced into an open war unless she desired it; she was not asked to put up any money or ships; she would have a scapegoat handy always; and finally she would have an excellent prospect of achieving untold wealth and power. The whole thing would be done by a private company, and she would be obliged to contribute nothing more substantial than a secret blessing upon the enterprise.

Still, it was strong stuff for her. Later, she was to grow accustomed to proposals of this sort, and to sanction them. But this first one gave her considerable pause. She was cautious, wary. Perhaps there were compromises; probably there were. Nevertheless, the fact remains that within a few months after the second discourse was submitted, Humphrey Gilbert suddenly was granted what he had been trying for many years, by other methods, to get—a charter authorizing him to assemble and equip a fleet and to plant a colony, of which he would be the governor, in the New World.

CHAPTER XVII

KNOLLYS BACKS OUT

THIS charter was the first of its sort, and it became the model for subsequent similar charters. As such, it is surely one of the most important single documents in the history of the British Empire, and it has been called the Magna Carta of Greater Britain.

It is not long. Gilbert himself probably wrote it—indeed, probably he had written it years earlier, in preparation. Not that it is in his usual easy style. On the contrary, it is stiff, encrusted with top-heavy phrases; even for those times, it is exceptionally replete with legalisms; whoever wrote it, Gilbert or another, wrote with an eye to future lawsuits, straining himself to include every phrase that might plug up any possible legal loophole. This fact is significant in view of the battle which raged for the rest of Humphrey Gilbert's life—and has been raging in the dusty pages of history ever since—as to whether the man ever truly intended to plant a colony in North America.

The charter gives to Sir Humphrey and his heirs and assigns forever "free liberty and license . . . to discover, find, search out, and view such remote, heathen and barbarous lands, countries and territories not actually possessed of any Christian prince or people . . . and the same to have, hold, occupy and enjoy to him, his heirs and assigns forever, with all commodities, jurisdictions and royalties both by sea and land."

The word "forever" is used repeatedly, but there is a paragraph which specifically provides that unless a colony is established within six years of the date of the granting of the charter, then the charter becomes void. This six-year provision, as you will learn, was a very important one.

The strict laws against fugitives from England—men who quit the country without the Queen's permission—were set aside as far as Humphrey Gilbert's colony is concerned; and he was given authority to take with him to the New World "such and so many of our subjects as shall willingly accompany him." In effect, it offered a free pardon to criminals who would go with Gilbert.

All the land was to be held by Humphrey Gilbert, and those to whom he should sell or assign it, in fee simple, "or otherwise, according to the order of the laws of England, as near as the same conveniently may be." All colonists were to enjoy the same legal rights as though they were resident within the boundaries of England itself. Sir Humphrey, as governor, was to be answerable only to the Queen. The government of the colony was to be in his hands, and he was to make it "as near as conveniently may be" like that of England; at least, its laws must not clash with any regular English laws; and of course, the Church of England must be the recognized church in the colony.

Provision was made against the possibility that the Spanish or French, claiming this land, might descend upon the settlement:

"And moreover, we do by these presents for us, our heirs and successors, give and grant licence to the said Sir Humphrey Gilbert, his heirs and assigns, and to every one of them, that he and they, and every and any of them shall, and may from time to time, and all times for ever hereafter, for his and their defence, encounter, expulse, repel and resist, as well by Sea as by land, and by all other ways whatsoever, all and every such person and persons whatsoever, as without the special licence and liking of the said Sir Humphrey, and of his heirs and assigns, shall attempt to inhabit within the said countries, or any of them, or within the space of two hundred leagues near to the place or places within such countries as aforesaid, if they shall not be before planted or inhabited within the limits aforesaid. . . ." In other words, if any foreigners tried to put them out, or got too close to them, they were authorized to fight. A war for defence only, of course, all other kinds of wars being evil.[1]

The Queen was to get her share: she was to receive outright one-fifth of all the gold and silver that might be found. In common with most other contemporary Europeans, educated and otherwise, she believed that America was a vast storehouse of gold and silver, which might be had for the mere trouble of picking it up and bringing it back. The delusion is not difficult to understand when the experiences of Cortez, Pizarro, and their successors are considered.

There was to be one preliminary voyage for the purpose of finding a place to settle, and then another voyage for the purpose of settling there. The charter refers to "this journey of discovery, or in the second journey for conquest hereafter." This had been a part of Gilbert's plan for some time.

Then came this significant paragraph:

"Provided always, and our will and pleasure is, and we do so hereby declare to all Christian Kings, princes and states, that if the said Humphrey, his heirs or assigns, or any of them, or any other by their licence or

---

[1] The particular sentence of which this is only a part contains 384 words, one colon, no semi-colons, and seven times the phrase "Sir Humphrey, his heirs and assigns." Nor is this by any means the longest sentence in the charter. The fact is mentioned not as a criticism of the author's style, nor as a jibe at the pomposity of legal phraseology, but simply to show the painstaking care which must have gone into the preparation of this document. The thing must have been written over and over again.

appointment, shall at any time or times hereafter rob or spoil by Sea or by land, or do any act of unjust and unlawful hostility to any of the Subjects of us, our heirs, or successors, or any of the Subjects of any King, prince, ruler, governor or state being then in perfect league and amity with us, our heirs or successors: and that upon such injury, or upon just complaint of any such prince, ruler, governor or state, or their subjects, we, our heirs or successors, shall make open proclamation within any of the ports of our Realm of England commodious, that the said Sir Humphrey, his heirs or assigns, or any other to whom these our Letters patents may extend, shall within the term to be limited by such proclamations, make full restitution and satisfaction of all such injuries done, so as both we and the said Princes, or others so complaining, may hold us and themselves fully contented." If restitution is not made, the charter provides, the offending parties will be disowned by England and might be "pursued in hostility" by any nation interested—in other words, they would become complete outcasts, acknowledged pirates, men without a country.

Observe that Elizabeth, or Gilbert, anticipated complaints from Spain, she specifically asserting "to all Christian Kings, princes and states" that she will not tolerate piracy or any other unlawful activity. They knew that Spain would take alarm.

And of course Spain did. Bernardino de Mendoza, the Spanish ambassador at St. James's, an arrogant, hot-headed fellow, objected immediately. His nation had for a long time, and with good reason, been suspicious of Sir Humphrey Gilbert and all Sir Humphrey's troublesome cousins. And Mendoza had spies in high places. Probably he knew about the discourses on "annoying" the King of Spain, in spite of the efforts to keep those documents a close secret. Certainly he knew in advance that Elizabeth was going to grant Sir Humphrey the colonization charter.

Sir Humphrey himself knew this. It is a fact worth remembering in any discussion concerning Sir Humphrey's true intentions. The business of getting together a large fleet in those days required about half a year; yet a few months after the charter had been granted—at Westminster, June 11, 1578—Humphrey Gilbert had assembled and provisioned his ships, eleven in number, had enlisted and armed and instructed his men, and was ready to go.

He was a hard worker, familiar with this type of job, and he was assisted by enthusiastic friends, but he could not have completed so big a task in so short a time. He must have known, many months in advance, and known for certain, that this latest petition of his was going to be granted.

We learn from Mendoza, indeed, that Humphrey Gilbert had four ships manned and provisioned for some time before the letters-patent were granted. Mendoza, of course, had his spies watching those ships; he knew as well as anybody else in England—better than most—that something was going to happen soon. On June 3rd, more than a week before Elizabeth had formally granted the colonization charter, Mendoza was writing to King Philip concerning those ships of Gilbert's, which, he said, were to be joined later by others. "It is believed that when they are out at sea, they will . . . go towards the Indies, unless," added the ambassador suggestively, "there be some disturbance in Ireland or Scotland which should detain them." For Philip was by no means above indulging in a little "underhand war" himself, and the Irish rebels had for some time been importuning him to lend them money and fighting-men. Like Elizabeth, when she dealt with the Huguenots and the Dutch rebels, Philip, in dealing with the Irish, would not commit himself officially; like her, he disavowed the troops he sent to Ireland; and like her, again, he masked his "underhand war" beneath a perfectly transparent cloak of religion.

"They are taking with them a Portuguese called Simon Fernandez, a great rogue, who knows that coast well, and has given them much information about it," continues Mendoza in the same letter. He adds that he is having Fernandez shadowed.

Humphrey Gilbert had thrown himself whole-heartedly into the task before him. But it was proving more difficult than he had expected. He was loyally backed by his friends and relatives: the list of investors in the enterprise is studded with the name of brothers, half-brothers, or cousins, such as Sir John Gilbert, Walter Raleigh, George Carew, Adrian Gilbert, Charles Champernoun, George Carew of Okington, Carew Raleigh, and others, and old acquaintances such as William Hawkins, Sir George Peckham, Sir Edward Horsey. But his enemies were almost as numerous and they were at least as determined. Mendoza's men were everywhere, blocking this, hindering that, stirring up dissension among the adventurers, starting lawsuits upon any sort of excuse.

His own second-in-command, Henry Knollys, gave him great trouble. Knollys was a conceited fellow, a relative of the Queen on her mother's side and inordinately proud of this fact. He estimated himself to be worthy twenty knights such as Humphrey Gilbert, and he said so, publicly. Why he went into the venture in the first place it is difficult to understand. If he had been in Mendoza's pay he could not have acted in a manner better calculated to please that Spaniard.

He quarrelled with Gilbert. He won to his side one of Gilbert's cousins, Richard Denny, who had been irked when the admiral ventured to discipline him. So as siduously did he stir up hard feeling between Gilbert and Denny that Denny went so far as to challenge the admiral to a duel—a challenge Sir Humphrey appears to have ignored.

Then some of Knollys' sailors, ashore at Plymouth, got drunk and killed a man. They took refuge on their ship; and when the Lord Lieutenant of Devonshire demanded that they be surrendered to him, Knollys refused to deliver them. This caused further trouble and delay. Gilbert went to London, presumably in an effort to straighten the matter, and in his absence Knollys quarrelled with one of the ship captains, Miles Morgan, a staunch adherent of the admiral. Knollys, as acting admiral, went so far as to sentence Morgan to death, and he was engaged in making preparations for a hanging on shipboard when Sir Humphrey returned from the capital. Sir Humphrey released and reinstated his friend Morgan, and Knollys retired to his cabin in a huff. In an effort to patch up matters with his second-in-command, Sir Humphrey sent him an invitation to dinner. Knollys refused to accept the invitation, and his refusal was couched in insulting language.

Sir Humphrey kept his temper; but it was probably a distinct relief when at last Knollys decided to desert altogether, and sailed off, with Denny, taking with him four of the eleven ships. Materially this weakened the fleet. Actually, it probably strengthened the fleet. At any rate, it did not turn the admiral from his purpose. He wrote promptly to Walsingham, one of his best friends at Court, that he still was prepared to go about the business he had undertaken—though in this letter, as in all other letters of the time, he carefully refrained from stating the nature of that business.

CHAPTER XVIII

A HUSHED-UP AFFAIR

IT IS instinctive for a biographer to protect and defend his subject. That subject may have been in a grave for centuries; but the biographer, if he be conscientious and honest, has lived with the man, thought with him, thrilled with him in adventure, troubled with him in adversity. He knows the man. Often he knows him better than he knows his own neighbours and relatives, better than he knows the persons he meets every day, and talks with, and dines with, and lives with.

So that he is that man's very close friend. And when he knows the man to be wrong, he loves him still, and admires him; and when he merely *suspects* the man to be wrong, he quite naturally moves to give him the benefit of the doubt.

This is particularly true of Humphrey Gilbert, who, himself one of the loyalest men who ever lived, inspires a corresponding loyalty in anybody who gets really acquainted with him.

But impartiality is a stern obligation set upon the biographer; and that phrase "benefit of the doubt," paradoxically, has too many meanings to mean anything.

There *is* doubt, worlds of doubt, about this first voyage of Sir Humphrey Gilbert. To this day, in spite of the tireless research of many learned men over a period of many years, we do not know where the knight intended to go when he set out, or what he intended to do. The statesmen, this time, managed to keep their secret not only from those immediately charged with getting it, but also from all posterity. The utmost mystery surrounds the whole business. Even private letters give us no clue. Even the most reliable and usually most thorough of narrators, such as Hakluyt, supply not one hint. Mendoza himself, though he strove with every means at his command, could not learn the purpose and destination of this assembling fleet. He had his suspicions, as historians have had theirs, but of true proof, or certain knowledge, he had none.

The very circumstance that such extraordinary care was taken to keep secret the facts concerning the fleet does much to bolster the belief held by Mendoza, that this was nothing more than a disguised piratical expedition. Humphrey Gilbert's amazing proposal to "annoy" the King of Spain, in which he specifically suggested a raiding fleet masked as a colonization expedition, and the promptitude with which this petition was acted upon by a monarch habitually vacillating, and also the fact that Sir Humphrey was making definite preparations so far in advance and was so extremely eager to be off as soon as possible after the granting of the colonization charter,—all these circumstances help to strengthen the belief.

There is the additional fact that even after the desertion of Knollys and Denny, the fleet was a powerful one and well armed at all points. There were, then, seven ships. The flagship, the *Ann Ager*, named after Lady Gilbert, was of 250 tons burden, and she carried 29 pieces of cannon and 126 "gents, soldiers and mariners," besides the admiral, master, and officers. The other vessels were likewise heavily armed. In all, there were 525 men, including a large number of professional soldiers, and more than 100 assorted cannon. Surely all this was not required for the simple purpose of seeking a place in a savage country in which to settle at a later date?

Knowing her methods, we need not take too seriously Elizabeth's strict injunction against buccaneering and other forms of lawless behavior. The greatest thief of all times was Francis Drake, who, when he had returned from his sensational trip around the world after sacking dozens of ships and dozens of cities, and while all Spain was clamoring for his execution, was calmly knighted by a grateful and wealthier Queen. Between the public promises and private performances of Elizabeth, it is perhaps needless to repeat, there was often a great gulf. That precautionary paragraph in the colonization charter was, after all, nothing but a public promise—as Humphrey Gilbert must have known, having himself proposed its inclusion in the document.

It seems fair enough, then, to suppose that Humphrey Gilbert, on this first voyage, really was not going to Newfoundland for the purpose of exploration and the selection of a site for an English settlement. He may have hoped to do that, too, but it could not have been his sole object, or even his principal one.

Still, I defend my friend. He may have been turning pirate for the time because it would better his grand scheme of making the New World English; or he may have been turning pirate chiefly because it would better the condition of his own pocketbook. But is it logical that a man who had dreamed colonization, argued it, studied it, laboured for it, for twenty years, would abruptly dump all his cherished ambitions overboard and sally forth as a simple despoiler of Spaniards? Is there any sense in the suggestion, solemnly advanced by some historians, that all this planning and hoping and writing and working—a lifetime of it—all was for the purpose of promoting one vast piratical expedition? Is there anything about the life of the author of the *Discourse of the Northwest Passage* to indicate that he was the sort of man who would waste a lifetime deceiving the world as to his true intentions in order to gain one glorious opportunity to rob? For that matter, is there anything about the Queen, about the Court, calculated to make one believe that any pirate of the time *needed* to go to so much trouble?

No, I think that the dream of the north-west passage, the dream of English colonies in America and of a rich trade with the Orient, still was strong in Humphrey Gilbert's breast—stronger, it may be, than ever. It is not possible, even, that he had become discouraged, disgusted, and had seized upon this voyage as a means of filling his purse and enhancing his prestige at Court, the while he discarded his original ambition. It is not possible, simply because he was not that sort of man. I can vouch for it. I know him well.

The delays exacerbated him. They delighted the Spanish ambassador, to whom they gave an opportunity to institute further causes for delay. "I have sent a man expressly to make the voyage with Humphrey Gilbert, so that if he returns, he will give a full account of it to me," Mendoza wrote to Philip on August 14th, while Sir Humphrey still was striving to straighten matters and push out to sea. "I have been fortunate in finding a person both faithful and competent, he being an Englishman, and if they should touch in Spain on their return, he is to go straight to Court and address himself to you."

Besides the Knollys trouble and the obstructions raised by Mendoza, the weather was all against the enterprise from the first. The fleet was assembling at Dartmouth, but headwinds held back some of the ships which were due from London.

Finally, however, the fleet was assembled, seven ships.

The flagship, the *Ann Ager*, bore as her motto the

same words Humphrey Gilbert had placed below his own coat-of-arms: *Quid Non?* ("Why Not?").

The vice-admiral, the *Hope of Greenway*, was commanded by Carew Raleigh. The Queen's own material contribution, the *Falcon*,[1] 100 tons, was commanded by Walter Raleigh, who, like his half-brother, the admiral, was about to have his first trip to sea. Her motto was a bold one—*Nec mortem peto nec finem fugio* ("I neither fear death nor flee the end"). Simon Fernandez was aboard this ship, and he may have been "a great rogue," as Mendoza alleges, but certainly he was a valuable member of such a party as this. The *Red Lion*, 110 tons, was in charge of that same Miles Morgan whom Knollys had intended to hang. The others were the *Gallion*, 40 tons; the *Swallow*, 40 tons; and an incredibly tiny frigate, the *Squirrel*, grossing 8 tons only and carrying eight men, officers and crew.

So they sailed, September 26th, from Dartmouth. They left a welter of trouble behind them, but they managed to find more of it ahead. It was a bad time of the year for sallying out of England. Gales dispersed the fleet, and it reassembled, taking refuge at the Isle of Wight. From there it sailed on October 29th, but it was forced back soon afterward to Plymouth. It made again for the Isle of Wight, and sailed from there, finally, on November 19th. It touched at Ireland a little later, but where, and just when, we do not know. And then, at last, it definitely put to sea.

Some time later the ships returned. If the taking-off

---

[1] It is still another bit of evidence in support of the theory that Sir Humphrey was not going north to settle but rather was going south to steal, that the Queen contributed a "tall ship." Elizabeth not infrequently contributed ships of her own to adventuring fleets, thus becoming a stockholder in the venture; but she did this only when there was a possibility of immediate material gain; there is no instance on record of her contributing ships or money toward any purely pioneering project.

was shrouded in mystery, the coming-back was Mystery itself. Here the exasperated historian encounters a blank wall. It is almost unbelievable that such a fleet could set out on such a mission—whatever the mission was, surely it was an important one—and return, leaving no clue as to where it had been. But this is the case. The affair was thoroughly hushed up. Every chink through which a wee beam of light might be expected to shine had been carefully plugged; and there is nothing to do about it but guess.

We do not even know *when* the ships came back. The first and almost the only record of their return comes from that usually excellent source of information, the Spanish ambassador, who wrote to his king on February 22, 1579, three months after the sailing: "Humphrey Gilbert and Knollys have returned . . . and the man I sent with them has returned." Only this, and nothing more.

One ship didn't come back at all. This was the *Red Lion*, which, with her captain, Miles Morgan, and her crew, was left somewhere at the bottom of the Atlantic. Again there are no details at all.

Richard Hakluyt, whose whole life was devoted to the careful recording of just such voyages as this one, and who was himself intensely interested in Sir Humphrey and his enterprise, usually can be relied upon to supply information not elsewhere available; he was an uncommonly conscientious man, Hakluyt. But of the first Gilbert expedition Hakluyt had no more to say than that "it began, continued, and ended adversely."

Of official reports there were none—or if there were any, they have been lost or destroyed.

Many historians have stated that the ships went direct to Newfoundland, but because of the season, or because of weather and other troubles, were obliged to return promptly without having accomplished anything.

It is not likely. In the first place, it is not likely that they ever were intended for Newfoundland. Various reasons in support of this belief have already been given here. There was an additional reason in the presence of Simon Fernandez, a skilled navigator in the southern seas, but not at all familiar with northern waters, where problems of navigation are quite different. It is possible that the intention was to go to Florida and then work up north along the coast, looking for a good place to establish a colony: this is what Fernandez later did for Walter Raleigh, when Raleigh was carrying on his half-brother's work and attempting to establish the first English colony in the New World. But even that, in this case, is hardly likely; for the experiences of Frobisher and others already must have made it clear that sailing the northern seas at that time of the year—it was late November when the expedition really got started—would be suicide, nothing less.

Again, there is one vague hint of a sea battle with the Spaniards. John Hooker, in an address to Walter Raleigh, some years later, refers obscurely to the first Gilbert expedition: "Infinite commodities in sundry respects would have ensued from that voyage, if the fleet then accompanying you, had according to appointment followed you; or yourself had escaped the dangerous sea-fight, wherein many of your company was slain, and your ships therewith also sore battered and disabled."

This has led some writers to assume, without any further authority, that there was a battle with the Spaniards—a battle from which the Englishmen emerged second best. It is scarcely probable. Even in those days there were not pitched battles at sea between fleets representing two great nations without *some* official record being made thereof. Certainly Mendoza would have heard of such a battle, and certainly he would have utilized the news to cry, "Pirate!" at Humphrey Gilbert. Mendoza was throwing himself with delight into this task of crying "Pirate!" Any excuse was sufficient. Humphrey Gilbert was down, and Mendoza was kicking him, determined to take advantage of the situation, determined to prevent this dangerous man from getting to his feet again. Be sure that if there had been a seafight, Mendoza would have made the most of it.

Hooker is ordinarily a reliable chronicler, which makes this quotation the more puzzling. It is possible, I think, that when he wrote the much-discussed passage quoted above he was using a figure of speech and was referring not to a battle with another human force, but to a fight with heavy seas and stormy weather. That Gilbert's ships encountered the worst sort of weather we *do* know.

Edward Haies, who wrote very fully the details of the second Gilbertian expedition to the New World, and who may have been a member of this first expedition—who would have been familiar with it, anyway, for he was a ship-owner and well acquainted personally with Gilbert and others associated with him—records of it only that Sir Humphrey "adventured to sea, when having tasted of no less misfortune he was shortly after driven to retire home with the loss of a tall ship, and more to his grief a valiant gentleman Miles Morgan."

Haies is a dependable witness, a careful, God-fearing man. If there had been a fight against the Spaniards, certainly he would have mentioned the fact.

Apparently what happened was nothing so dramatic. Apparently the seven ships, after repeated difficulties in getting started at all, eventually were dispersed by the continuous gales, and were forced to put back to English ports in whatever order they could—or in no order at all. This procedure would not have been without precedent. I think we are safe in assuming that Humphrey

Gilbert got nowhere on this trip, and did nothing whatever.

His genius for failure had not deserted him. But so far from being dismayed, immediately he started plans to push off again. He did not even wish to wait until the spring. He insisted that he was not finished—that he had not even started.

But now it was too late. Speed was what he had needed more than any other one thing, once Elizabeth had agreed to give her blessing to the venture. He himself had understood this; he had wished to get away as soon as the charter was granted. Most of the delays, we know, were not his fault. Certainly he could not be blamed for the weather, which was extraordinarily bad that fall and winter on the north Atlantic. Possibly some of the fault was his. Possibly he was not a good manager for such an undertaking. Book learning, great zeal, and perfect courage are not sufficient, of course. Perhaps the armchair sailor should have essayed a few shorter trips first, before he assumed control of a whole fleet.

Every delay was a gain for the enemy. Mendoza himself was alert enough, and knew what to do; but Mendoza's master was a hopeless plodder, behindhand in everything he tried. A hastily promoted uprising in Ireland, such as the ambassador had suggested, would have prevented Humphrey Gilbert from sailing in the first place, charter or no charter; for Elizabeth never was willing to let any of her fighting-men go away when there was the slightest hint of trouble near home. King Philip acted upon his ambassador's suggestion, but he was characteristically slow about it. But then, Sir Humphrey was slower still.

Now that Sir Humphrey was back, the Spanish opposition was fully organized, an "underhand war" had been inaugurated on the Emerald Isle, and Mendoza was making objections and filing lawsuits at a high rate of speed, entangling the admiral in all sorts of litigation, and frightening the Queen.

So for all his eagerness to be off again, for all his grand plans, for all his boundless confidence and hard courage, Sir Humphrey was instructed to remain in England. Never mind the letters-patent; this colonization business could be put over for a more propitious time.

In April, after a period of Mendoza's most expert bullying, the Privy Council wrote to Sir Humphrey instructing him to put up large sureties for himself and his associates, "to refrain from any piratical action," if he desired to sail again. He couldn't do it. He didn't have the money. He had put into the expedition all his own money, mortgaging or selling everything he possessed. He likewise had sunk his wife's entire fortune into the business. Faced with a multitude of lawsuits and with his own two ships taken over by the government for service in Ireland, in spite of his protests, he simply could not raise that money.

The Spanish ambassador charged that Gilbert had stopped a Spanish ship in Walfled Bay and stolen her cargo of oranges. He demanded restitution. He charged that the expedition had landed in Galacia, where the men sacked a village and a monastery. Again he demanded restitution.

It is improbable that these acts ever occurred. Gilbert himself denied all knowledge of them, and there is no record to show that the cases ever were pushed to their conclusion in the courts. But meanwhile, they had served their purpose. Humphrey Gilbert was ordered back to Ireland. Ireland!

CHAPTER XIX

"THE MASTER THIEF OF THE UNKNOWN WORLD"

THE seemingly unquashable James FitzMaurice was in open rebellion again. He had three ships, and with these he was raiding English merchant vessels off the coast of Cornwall. In addition, a small force of Spanish and Italian soldiers, ostensibly sent by the Pope but actually sent by King Philip, had landed at Smerwick, in Ireland, and was engaged in giving assistance and encouragement to rebellious Irishmen in those parts.

The two ships Humphrey Gilbert still owned were almost his only assets now, and these were taken over by the government, and the knight was commissioned to "pursue, punish, correct and plague the said James Fitz-Maurice." Another petty job—another cheap, stupid little war. The eagle was back in its cage; and Cathay still was very, very far away, beyond the blue horizon.

Evidently he did not undertake this job personally, or if he did so, it was only for a time. Mostly, it appears, he was living quietly in London during all this fuss, and deputies were carrying on the Irish work, using Sir Humphrey's ships and supplies and cannon and powder. Oh yes, the government was to reimburse him for the use of these things! But he knew well enough what a task it was to get money out of the government, however just the claim.

The following autumn Francis Drake returned from his trip around the world, the most glamorous piratical undertaking of all times. There was no Plimsoll's Mark in those days; and when the gallant *Golden Hind* sailed up the Channel she was so loaded with gold and silver and jewels, loot from Spanish cities thousands of miles away, that she was scarcely able to stay afloat. There were millions in the hold of that ship. Englishmen had never before seen such treasure, had scarcely even dared to dream of it.

Of course, Francis Drake was a rank thief. Without any excuse, without any authority, charter, letters-patent, or anything of the sort, this amazing little redhead had leapt upon city after city, town after town, ship after Spanish ship, in the New World; and right joyously he had robbed and plundered, burnt and despoiled. And now he was back with his profits.

Those profits were staggering. It scarcely seemed possible, but it is a matter of cold record that shareholders in this particular enterprise of Drake's got 4,700 per cent. return on their investments!

Now obviously a man who could sally out of England and return with such a cargo as that was a much more important person than a man who dreamed grand dreams of establishing empires. Drake never troubled himself about empires.[1] He was purely and simply a robber—a magnificent robber, and one of the greatest masters of amphibious warfare the world has ever known.

[1] One of Drake's earlier companions, John Oxenham, in or about 1574 testified before the Spanish Inquisition that Drake had often told him that if Queen Elizabeth would sanction the plan, he, Drake, would sail to the Magellan Straits and found settlements thereabouts. But we need not take this too seriously, in view of the agency of catechism. The Spanish Inquisition, it is tolerably well known, had machines calculated to make any witness testify just about what the inquisitors desired him to testify; and an ambition to colonize in South America would be, in Spanish eyes, another grave charge against "El Draque" ("The Dragon"), as they called Drake. Certainly Drake never formally petitioned the Queen to establish such colonies; his name never was associated with any colonization project, however remotely; and there is nothing in his whole life that would indicate that he was interested in the Americas as anything but a place for robbing Spaniards.

Spain, wailing, bleating, demanded his head. But you just can't lop off the head of a man who shows a 4,700 per cent. return on an investment—especially in view of the fact that the Queen herself had been one of the shareholders. An inexcusable thief he was, yes. But he was also a very profitable subject. Elizabeth not only failed to punish him: she attended a dinner aboard the *Golden Hind*, and when the eating was finished she knighted the host—*Sir* Francis Drake thereafter, if you please.

He was perhaps the most discussed man in Europe at the time, this "master thief of the Unknown World"; and he loved it, he gloried in it. Short, stocky, with bright blue eyes, and a spatulate beard appropriately red, Sir Francis not only led a dramatic life, but he behaved, personally, in a dramatic manner. He knew the value of display; he was altogether magnificent, incredibly picturesque.

The importance of this two-year trip around the world was great. For one thing, it gave England her first big slice of the riches of the Americas. For another, it turned the thoughts of men toward the sea, stimulating all sorts of ambitions, loosening capital, increasing the prestige of the master mariner and the student of navigation and of geography. Then, too, it brought Spain and England inevitably closer to open warfare—though neither Elizabeth nor King Philip had any desire for an open fight. At the English Court, it strengthened incalculably the position of the anti-Spanish party, of which Sir Humphrey Gilbert was such a prominent member. And it made the Spaniards more fiercely determined than ever to resist all efforts to snatch from them the Americas with their untold wealth.

However, the feature of this greatest of piratical expeditions in which Sir Humphrey Gilbert was most interested was Drake's attempt to return to England by way of the north-west passage, in the existence of which he, too, utterly practical mariner that he was, apparently believed. Drake, as everybody knows, sailed through the Straits of Magellan and into the Pacific Ocean, the first Englishman ever to accomplish this feat. Gleefully he sacked the unsuspecting Spanish towns and trading-posts along the western coast of South America and Central America; and then, laden with all the riches he could possibly carry, he was faced with the problem of how to get home again. He could not go back through the Straits of Magellan. The Spaniards, completely surprised on the west coast, when the alarm was raised had hastened to block those straits against his return; they were waiting there for him in overwhelming numbers.

Faced with this problem, Drake continued north, intent upon returning by way of that north-west passage Humphrey Gilbert was forever talking about. He got as far north as the forty-eighth degree of latitude, or about opposite the site of the present city of Vancouver, B. C. Then he turned back; and eventually he returned to England by following the route of the only other man who had sailed around the world, Magellan.

Why Drake turned back we do not know. He himself said that the extreme cold forced him to do so. This does not sound plausible; for it was midsummer, and the neighbourhood of Vancouver at that time of the year, even to men whose blood had been thinned by long sailing in tropic seas, could not have seemed dangerously cold. Mr. E. F. Benson suggests that Drake's real reason for turning back was the fact that his charts were hopelessly inaccurate, or possibly even the fact that his crew was muttering mutiny. We have no certain knowledge of this. What Humphrey Gilbert was interested in, and what we are interested in here, is the fact that Francis Drake believed in the existence of that north-west passage. It is unfortunate that he did not seek it further. If *he* had been unable to find it, then surely it did not exist; and if this fact had been established in 1580, many a good English life would have been spared.

While we have Drake here, let's examine him. You get to know a man not only by studying him, but also by studying the men who surround him, and particularly by contrasting him with his opposites. Drake and Gilbert, side by side, make an exceptionally interesting pair. Drake, a commoner, small, compact, essentially practical, was one of the most successful men who ever lived; he knew what he wanted, and he went out and got it. The tall, aristocratic Gilbert, as we have seen, was a born, a foredoomed failure. Drake was a man of action and never a dreamer. Gilbert also was a man of action; but first of all he was a dreamer.

Much more significant is a comparison of their methods of planning, their preparations, and their aims. Drake was wholly destructive. It is true that he was, perhaps, a good thing for England: it is, at any rate, debatable. But this was not because he *aimed* to be a good thing for England. His exploits were so sensational, and so lucrative, that they stimulated lagging English interest in the sea; they fired men with ambitions to sail to the New World. But this effect was an incidental offspring of Drake's real purpose.

Whereas Gilbert, even in his wildest schemes, had some constructive purpose in mind. Always he desired to better England, enlarge England, glorify England. It may be that he was not averse to filling his own pocketbook in the process; but if gain, and nothing but gain, had been his sole motive, as it was Drake's sole motive, he would never have done the things he did—nor could he have conceived the greater things that he meant to do. Observe that Drake struck and departed, leaving ashes, panic; but Gilbert proposed to strike and capture, to keep, to rebuild, to settle, to make the Spanish domains permanently English.

But then, Drake succeeded while Gilbert failed; and *that* difference interests the world at large more than any other.

Gilbert is a very quiet, very dim figure, for these next few years of English history. Elizabethans had little patience with a man who had missed. There wasn't time for studying the ultimate effect of things; there was too much to be grabbed immediately, without thought. So Humphrey Gilbert, who had failed, was discredited. He did not produce gold; and so he was, as much as possible, ignored. Vainly he petitioned for the money that the government owed him for the use of his two ships. Vainly he begged to be permitted to recoup his losses and make another try at colonization of the New World. He was unheeded. England wasn't interested.

Brother Walter, too, was sent to Ireland now; but he went as a soldier, not as a sailor. And he followed as closely as possible in brother Humphrey's Irish footsteps. He was present when the fort at Smerwick fell, and the miserable invading force of Spaniards and Italians, together with some 200 Irish men and women and children, refugees, surrendered. He was one of the two captains sent into Smerwick to put the entire garrison to the sword. Walter Raleigh was a soldier, and he did a thorough job—the sort of job his half-brother would have done under the circumstances. Nobody emerged alive. For this was "underhand war," in which quarter was not given and not expected. There was nothing unusual about this. Some historians, subsequently, have become highly indignant about it; but Walter Raleigh wasn't indignant, nor was Humphrey Gilbert, nor was anybody else at the time. Certainly Elizabeth did not object. Though she was in full possession of all the gruesome details, she wrote a letter to the commander of the

English force, Lord Grey of Wilton, commending him for his action, and blaming him only for his failure to spare the few foreign officers, who, she pointed out, might have been ransomed.

Brother Walter, believing in brother Humphrey's measures and methods, sought to emulate him. There is a marked similarity between these two men, who were such fast friends. But brother Walter had a dash of Drake in him; he was a dreamer, yes, but he was a hard-bitten man of the world, too; his ambition was boundless; he was keen, alert, ready for success, and accepting success, when it came to him, as though it were only his just deserts. Brother Walter would go far. He was that kind of man.

He brought back to the Queen's attention the "undertaker" plan for colonization of Ireland with Englishmen, the same plan Humphrey Gilbert had urged some years previous. He had better success than Sir Humphrey, and got a large grant of land in Ireland.

But for his half-brother, his friend, Walter Raleigh had the liveliest appreciation. Writing to Walsingham in indignation about the comparative clemency of the current Lord Lieutenant of Ireland, himself an Irishman,[2] he said:

"What by reason of the incomparable hatred between him [the Lord Lieutenant] and the Geraldines, who will rather die a thousand deaths, enter into a million of mischiefs and seek succour of all nations, rather than they will ever be subdued by a Butler—that after Her Majesty hath spent a hundred thousand pounds more

[2] This was Thomas Butler, Earl of Ormond, Governor of Munster and General of the Forces in Ireland. He was chief of the Butlers; and of course the Geraldines weren't going to stand for *that*! Whenever anybody else started a fight in their part of the island, for whatever reason, the Geraldines and the Butlers used it as an excuse for renewing their ancient feud; and now they were at it again. This letter was written from Cork, February 25, 1581.

she shall at last be driven by too dear experience to send an English President to follow these malicious traitors with fire and sword, neither respecting the alliance nor the nation." Humphrey Gilbert's attitude again, you observe! And now comes a specific "boost" for brother Humphrey: "Would God your Honor and Her Majesty, as well as my poor self, understands how pitifully the service here goeth forward! Considering that this man, having now been Lord General of Munster about two years, there are at this instant a thousand traitors more than there were the first day. Would God the service of Sir Humphrey Gilbert might be rightly looked into; who, with the third part of the garrison now in Ireland, ended a rebellion not much inferior to this, in two months! Or would God his own behaviour were such in peace as it did not make his good service forgotten and hold him from the preferment he is worthy of! I take God to witness I speak not for affection but to discharge my duty to Her Majesty; for I never heard nor read of any man more feared than he is among the Irish nation. And I do assuredly know that the best about the Earl of Desmond, yea! and all the unbridled traitors of these parts, would come in here, and yield themselves to the Queen's mercy, were it but known that he were come among them. The end shall prove this to be true."

So! Ten years and more after he had quit Ireland, the Irish still trembled at his name. Allowance should be made, to be sure, for the sympathies of the writer of this letter, despite his protestations of impartiality; for Walter Raleigh was as loyal to his relatives as Humphrey Gilbert.

Another significant thing about this letter is the mention it makes of Humphrey Gilbert's modesty. Now modesty never handicapped Walter Raleigh, one of the most arrogant, most conceited men who ever lived. But there seems no doubt that his half-brother was deficient in the art of *swagger*, then, as now, a very important attribute—perhaps an even more important attribute then than now. Men in Elizabeth's Court generally rose to high positions by means of their own abilities; they were a talented lot, those fellows. But frequently enough they *kept* their positions partly through plain, ordinary boasting, showmanship. It was the thing to do—to blow your own horn, and blow it hard, and never to stop blowing it while you had a breath of air left in your lungs and a pumping heart in your breast. The Queen loved display. Raleigh, Leicester, Essex, Drake, all of her favourites, were men able to make a great show of everything they did; and not one of them was afflicted, as Humphrey Gilbert seems to have been, with the drawback of modesty. It seems to have been a handicap Humphrey Gilbert simply could not overcome. And so, on this as on other occasions, brother Walter, who had egotism to spare, did a little helpful boasting for him.

CHAPTER XX

DESIGNING ARCADIA

WALTER RALEIGH did not remain long in Ireland. Like other Englishmen sent there, soon after his arrival he began pulling political strings calculated to get him out; but unlike so many others, he succeeded. Back in London, he was the principal exponent of the Irish colonization plan, and one of those who derived the greatest benefit from the launching of that plan. He became, in effect, the government's Irish expert; he did more, perhaps, than any other man of his time to influence official English policy in regard to Ireland; the Privy Council invariably called him in for consultation when Ireland was discussed.

But then, this was to be expected of brother Walter, who was bound to rise and who would have glittered in any age and in any country in which he had happened to be born. Now in his lower thirties, extremely handsome, tall, straight, alert, clever, he was attracting the favourable notice of a middle-aged monarch who was staring rather more frankly at good-looking men than she had been wont to stare when she was younger and less firmly seated upon the throne.

Yes, brother Walter would have been a great man at any time and in any place. But he was fortunate in being born to shine under Elizabeth; for his greatness was peculiarly Elizabethan; he perfectly fitted his time. His talents were astounding; he was one of the most versatile men who ever lived. He was suave, arrogant, extravagant, a really great poet and prose writer, an excellent soldier, the Beau Brummel of his age, illimitably ambitious, and afraid of nothing. Of course Elizabeth purred when this splendid creature made love to her. Of course she loosened, at least a bit, that "frenzied grasp upon her money-bags." It was very difficult to keep anything from Walter Raleigh when once that accomplished gentleman felt a desire for it.

For all his activities—and the extent and variety of them is amazing—brother Walter always had time to help further the interests of brother Humphrey. Their relative positions at Court had been reversed, and it was the younger man, a Somebody now, no longer an obscure hanger-on, who was helping Sir Humphrey. For Sir Humphrey was something of a veteran courtier now, one who remembered the old days before Elizabeth ascended the throne—a veteran, yes, and rather a discredited veteran, too, whom few men took seriously any longer. But Walter Raleigh took him seriously. Walter Raleigh, from the very beginning, was heart and soul with his half-brother in the colonization schemes. He took a tremendous interest in navigation, though, like Sir Humphrey, he was rather an armchair sailor than an active seaman. He designed a new type of sailing-vessel. He invested in privateering enterprises. He used all his newly acquired influence at Court in an attempt to promote the interests of his Devonshire relatives and their sea ventures.

Humphrey Gilbert was faced now not only with the problem of money—*that* was always with him—but also with the time element. That six-year proviso in the letters-patent, which had seemed liberal at first, began to look ominous. It would be terrible to have the charter run out and no colony established! to have that vast empire across the sea—that empire he had never even seen—snatched away from him! Frantic, he ran from man to man; he coaxed and he urged, he argued and he wheedled. But the capital was not forthcoming. A man who had tried once and failed, found it very difficult to interest investors in a second attempt. He had no money of his own, now, and his wife had none. He wrote pitifully to Walsingham, in July, 1581, that he had been reduced to such circumstances that he was obliged "to sell my wifes' clothes from her back." He begged again, and again in vain, that the government pay him what it owed him for his ships that were used in the Irish service—a matter of some £2,000. Of the ships he had possessed, himself, a few years earlier, only one remained—and that was the smallest of them all, the 8-ton *Squirrel*.

He knew that the men who did have money to invest were interested only in sea ventures which, like Drake's, would promise tremendous and immediate cash returns. He seems to have planned still to finance his proposed colony by means of a series of Drake-like raids in the West Indies. At least, Mendoza believed this, and wrote so informing King Philip. Sir Humphrey, the ambassador reported, planned to establish a base in Cuba and from there sally forth and attack the Spanish treasure galleons. For *such* an enterprise he should be able to raise capital; and the proceeds could be devoted to the establishment of that northern colony which was never absent from his mind.

But time was short, and there was no cash. To make matters worse, the Privy Council, after a long discussion of the matter, solemnly decided that Sir Humphrey's letters-patent were now null and void, since he had attempted to exercise them and had failed. He had worked for many years to get that charter; it and the nebulous rights it bestowed upon him were his only possessions. He managed finally to get the Council to reverse its own decision. Possibly this was done in response to a sharp word from the throne. We lack details, but

DESIGNING ARCADIA

it is evident that even our failure still retained some influence at Court.

And so, at any rate, the undiscouraged Sir Humphrey remained governor and sole owner of an enormous portion of that New World he had never even seen. Great tracts of land were his, on paper, could he but go and take them. He would be one of the most powerful lords in the world, if— Always if. Always his thought reverted to that colony and to the north-west passage. And tirelessly, with bulldog tenacity, he continued to lay grand plans and to talk with potential investors.

He hit upon the happy idea of selling great portions of this unfounded empire of his. He had already sold everything else he possessed.

Graciously, but presumably for a price, he made over to Dr. John Dee, that curious old mystic, all the lands north of the fiftieth parallel of latitude. He assigned a mere matter of 1,500,000 acres to his friend, Sir George Peckham; and the following month he assigned 3,000,000 acres to his friend Sir Philip Sidney, who, a year later, gave this land to Peckham. Certain other rights were assigned to Peckham also, and to his associate, Sir Thomas Gerrard.

Indeed, a lot of things could be done with that charter; for Sir Humphrey, after all, was legal custodian of inconceivable possibilities; and there were other dreamers in England, too. Now he found himself getting assistance, definite financial assistance, from a most unexpected quarter—from the leaders of the Roman Catholic party in England.

Sir George Peckham and Sir Thomas Gerrard both were wealthy. A man *had* to be wealthy in order to be openly a Roman Catholic in England then; for the fines were enormous, and excuses for imposing them were without number. A Catholic was fined for all sorts of things, and then he was thrown into prison anyway and obliged to buy his way out with huge bribes. Both Sir George and Sir Thomas had but recently emerged from London Tower. It was an expensive faith.

Queen Elizabeth herself was tolerant enough, or else she was indifferent; we don't know which was the case, and it makes no practical difference anyway. She strove to make England quietly and effectively Protestant; and in the beginning of her reign, so long as the Catholics minded their own business and paid their fines, she did not trouble them—not, at least, in a manner comparable for an instant with the way Protestants were persecuted in Catholic nations at this time. And the English Catholics, appreciating this, paid their fines, refrained from meddling with politics, ignored the bull issued by Pius V in 1570, in which Elizabeth was proclaimed a rank heretic and no true queen at all, and, though it was against the law, celebrated mass all over the kingdom.

No, it was not the English Catholics themselves, men like Sir Thomas and Sir George, who spoiled this pleasant state of affairs. It was the interfering Catholics from the Continent, the zealots who dreamed still of bringing England back into Mother Church, and who were appearing in England in great numbers, preaching not merely religion, but also rebellion. From Elizabeth, they knew, they could expect nothing. Their only hope lay in stirring up rebellion. Most of them were Jesuits, from Cardinal Allen's seminary at Douai, and they believed that the end justified any means and were prepared to stop at nothing. Oh, they were honest and brave men! Personally they can be admired. But politically they were pests and they were becoming *dangerous* pests. In all fairness to Elizabeth, she was forced to take action against the Catholics. Her power depended wholly upon her Protestantism, and she knew it; she could not afford to tolerate missionaries grown bold. For Spain, of course, was backing these men with gold and other encouragement, and France was not above giving them a friendly word now and then. There were mutterings in Ireland, and in the north of England; and even in London there were plots against the Queen's life. King Philip himself had formally agreed that the best thing to be done about "this queen"—as she was invariably called in foreign courts—was to kill her.[1]

So the neglected anti-Catholic laws were dragged from their corners, dusted, and put back into operation; and an obliging Parliament passed some new laws imposing additional restrictions and fines. A few priests were burned, the government resolutely refusing to regard them as religious martyrs but insisting that they were mere traitors.

It was all very unfortunate. It gave the Spanish spies something more to work with, and it made matters very difficult for quiet, moderate men like Sir George and Sir Thomas and a multitude of lesser personages, who desired only to be permitted to remain good Catholics and good Englishmen at the same time.

Who it was who first suggested the remedy of shipping English Catholics to the New World, where they could worship as they pleased and still remain faithful to the English royal succession, we do not know. Perhaps Humphrey Gilbert went to Sir Thomas and Sir George with the proposal, or perhaps they came to him. A modern writer[2] has suggested that the scheme originated with Sir Francis Walsingham; and apparently Mendoza also held this opinion at the time—or desired to have it thought that he did; but there is no evidence to support it. Certainly Walsingham was interested in

[1] He said this quite openly, and the reason he gave is deliciously characteristic of the man. He said he desired the assassination of Elizabeth "not for my own interest, or for any other worldly object, but purely and simply for the service of God." The odd thing about this is that it probably was not hypocrisy at all, but the truth!

[2] R. B. Merriman, in the *American Historical Review*.

the scheme, and so was Sir Philip Sidney; and the veteran diplomat and the beloved young warrior-poet were powerful influences at Court just then. Oddly, both Walsingham and Sidney had records as ardent Catholic-haters. His biographer, Mr. Percy Addleshaw, finds his religious prejudice the one weakness in Sidney's otherwise admirable character; and glum old Walsingham was a strict Puritan, who disliked and distrusted Rome all his life. Yet here they were, a curious pair, coöperating in an effort to assist the English Catholics.

To complete this strange state of affairs, the principal opposition to the scheme came from the representative of the great Catholic champion, Philip of Spain. Mendoza objected loud and long. He objected officially, in Court, where he was not heeded; and he objected privately, among his Catholic friends, some of whom he managed to turn against the plan. He spread the rumour that this colonization scheme was nothing but a plot to get the Catholics out of England and desert them in the New World, where they would starve or be killed off by the savages. He wrote to his monarch: "I gave notice to the Catholics, through the priests who go among them, what are the real objects of the Queen and Council in extending this favour to them, and also that the country in question belonged to your Majesty and was defended by fortresses, so that directly they landed they would be slaughtered as Jean Ribault was."

The reference to Ribault was a shrewd one, for the memory of his fate was fresh. Ribault had been one of the Frenchmen who had attempted to settle some of his persecuted fellow Huguenots in the New World. They had planted a colony in what is now northern Florida. The greatest Spanish admiral of his time, Pedro Menendez, had leapt upon this colony and replaced it with a Spanish one. Menendez, a thoroughgoing sort of sailor, hanged every Huguenot, and around the neck of each corpse he suspended a placard which announced to all and sundry that this had been done not because the men were Frenchmen, but because they were pirates. The French later returned the compliment by obliterating the Spanish settlement, hanging every colonist with a placard around his neck announcing that this had been done not because the men were Spaniards, but because they were murderers. Nevertheless, Menendez had impressed his lesson upon the world; Spain had shown how she intended to treat foreigners who tried to occupy territory she considered her own; and the incident was a powerful deterrent to subsequent colonization plans, both in England and in France; the memory of it was one of the difficulties with which Sir Humphrey Gilbert had to contend when he went about promoting his own cherished plan.

It might be supposed that King Philip would be pleased to know that provision was being made to permit his fellow Catholics in England to worship as they desired. The contrary was true. For if there were no religious problem in England, then how could Philip hope to stir up trouble from time to time? What club would he have to use against Elizabeth, when a club was needed? Added to this was the fact that Sir Humphrey Gilbert was mixed up in the business; and anything in which Sir Humphrey was involved was, from Philip's point of view, a thing to be fought promptly.

But Elizabeth was favourably inclined, and the plan went ahead. Sir Humphrey conferred with this man and with that. He was becoming, again, an important person. He equipped two ships and sent them off on a "seeking-out" expedition, the results of which we do not know. He induced Walsingham to contribute £50. He accepted a liberal contribution from brother Walter, who planned to accompany the big expedition in person. He talked the bakers, brewers, tailors, yeomen, etc., of

Southampton, into investing £555 on the agreement that their city should be made the sole staple town for the New World. He had Hakluyt represent him in an appeal—but it was unsuccessful—to the governors of the Muscovy Company (the former Merchant Adventurers) at Bristol. He was careful to protect the interests of all those who had lost money on his first venture, making certain that they had their opportunity to invest in this second venture before others, outsiders, got in.

And on top of all that, he managed, at long last, to get some part—we do not know how much—of the money for which he had been dunning the government for many years.

He incorporated himself, selling stock in "The Merchant Adventurers with Sir Humphrey Gilbert." He laid the most elaborate plans for the governance of the new colony—for the distribution of lands, for the collection of rents and taxes, caring of bishops and archbishops, cultivation and fertilization of the soil, education of the young, provisioning and maintenance of an army and a navy, awarding of trade and fishing privileges, care of wounded soldiers, establishment of a library. . . .

"Sir Humphrey Gilbert's Commonwealth" was very real to him. He had worked it out to the last detail, having lived in that perfect land for many years—in his imagination. He had provided against everything, as he supposed. Forty-three years old, he was boundlessly enthusiastic. He would be the supreme head of the place, the life-long governor; and his children and their children would rule it after he had died. He would be the greatest lord of land in history—not, like Philip of Spain, by accident of birth the suzerain of distant territories he had not even seen and was obliged to rule through deputies—but an actual governor, living among his own people, sharing their problems, sharing their prosperity, in an Arcadia he himself had conceived, established, developed.

He appointed directors for his own corporation, and created Sir Francis Walsingham "Chief and Principal Patron" with authority to nominate successors if any should die or resign while Sir Humphrey himself was not in England. He made arrangements for the handling, in Southampton, of the goods he soon would be sending from the New World. He interested Burghley, Leicester, Warwick, Sussex, Christopher Hatton, and his former commander in Ireland, Sir Henry Sidney, and many other powerful personages. He wrote a will, on July 8, 1582—a curious, pathetic document, appointing Sir George Peckham, his brother Sir John Gilbert, and a brother-in-law, William Ager, trustees and executors, and leaving his wife and children large grants of land in the New World, besides large shares of the expected rentals and other forms of revenue. Poor Gilbert! he really believed he was providing well for his family. He was most careful to safeguard the interests of Lady Gilbert and the children against possible legal attack, and he was very generous with this land he hadn't seen and this princely income which still was mere paper and ink.

Then—when everything was in readiness for the beginning of the Great Adventure—came a letter from Walsingham reporting that the Queen objected to having Sir Humphrey leave the country. With characteristic bluntness, Elizabeth had stated that she didn't think much of Sir Humphrey as a sailor, and she liked him too much personally to have him risking his valuable life in a cockleshell on the stormy north Atlantic. He should stay at home, Elizabeth decreed.

This was a terrible blow. He was wild with anxiety. He knew that without Elizabeth's permission he could not make the trip, could not personally supervise the planting of the colony and govern it himself. The fact that he could do this *legally*, the fact that he had been granted letters-patent bearing Elizabeth's signature, meant nothing whatever to the Queen, who always insisted upon her royal and womanly right to change her mind at the last minute, and to break her word without any warning.

From his home in Red Cross Street, London, Sir Humphrey wrote an answer to Walsingham. It is dated February 7, 1582:

"Whereas it hath pleased your honour to let me understand that her majesty of her especial care had of my well doing, & prosperous success, hath wished my stay at home from the personal execution of my intended discovery as a man noted of no good hap by sea: for the which I acknowledge myself so much bounden unto her majesty, as I know not how to deserve the least part thereof, otherwise than with my continual prayer, and most faithful, and forward service during life: And now to excuse myself, and satisfy your honour touching the objections made of my stay, it may please you to be advertised that in my first enterprise I returned with great loss, because I would not myself, nor suffer any of my company to do anything contrary to my word given to her majesty and yourself: for if I had not far preferred my credit before my gain, I needed not to have returned so poor as then I did."

This statement, in view of the air of mystery with which that first enterprise was shrouded, is most interesting. Sir Humphrey carefully refrains, even here, from saying *what* it was that he had promised Elizabeth before setting sail, but the implication is that it was a promise to refrain from piracy. It is the only record—at least, the only one that has survived—of any defence made by him against the charges brought by Mendoza and others.

The delay, he asserts, was not his fault, but the fault of the winds and weather, which had been extraordinarily severe that winter. Discreetly (for this letter was only nominally written to Walsingham, and clearly was intended for the Queen herself) he remarks that Elizabeth is due to receive one-fifth of all the gold and silver found by his colonists, "without any charge to her majesty." He reviews the tremendous expense to which he had been put in attempting to establish a colony in America, "getting besides the scorn of the world, for conceiving so well of a matter that others hold so ridiculous, although now by my means better thought of."

Then the armchair sailor defends himself of the charge of being "a man noted of no good hap by sea."

"If the doubt be my want of skill to execute the same," he writes, "I will offer myself to be opposed by all the best navigators and cosmographers within the realm. If it be cowardliness, I seek no other purgation than my former service done to her majesty: if it be the suspicion of daintiness of diet or sea sickness, in these both I yield myself second to no man living, because that comparison is rather of hardiness of body than a boast of virtue."

Without any bombast, he reminds Elizabeth that he has served her faithfully and well for twenty-eight years, and he pleads with her, indirectly, to "allow me to get my living as well as I may honestly, which is every subject's right, and not to constrain me by my idle abode at home to beg my bread with my wife and children."

And he closes with an ardent and flowery batch of praises for Elizabeth, and the customary protestations of eternal devotion.

Then he sat down to wait. There was nothing else to do.

CHAPTER XXI

THE GREAT ADVENTURE BEGINS

THERE were other causes of delay, plenty of them. For one thing, there was the Muscovy Company. This group, of which Sir Humphrey himself had originally been a member, had done everything possible to thwart his plans from the very start. When first he had proposed to seek a north-west passage and to plant a colony in North America, the Muscovy Company—or the Merchant Adventurers, as the organization then was called—objected on the ground that *it* possessed exclusive exploration and trading privileges both north-west and north-east. It did nothing whatever to seek out a northwest passage, but neither was it willing to permit Humphrey Gilbert to do anything. And because of its previous charter, it was able to block his plans for many years.

When finally Sir Humphrey did obtain his own charter, the opposition included many members of the Muscovy Company. And when, after the first disastrous expedition, that charter had been revoked temporarily, it was the Muscovy Company officials who were largely responsible for this action.

And now, at last, when Gilbert was all but ready to embark, the Muscovy Company gentlemen suddenly agreed that the north-west plan was a sound one, after all, and, desperately anxious to keep Sir Humphrey from getting the credit for this, they proposed such an expedition themselves; they tried to steal his thunder.

He had appealed to them, through Hakluyt, to contribute to his expedition. They had refused. And then

Sir Humphrey, when he drew up his constitution for "The Merchant Adventurers with Sir Humphrey Gilbert," carefully wrote in a proviso that under no circumstances was any member of the Muscovy Company to be permitted to hold stock in this new company or benefit in any way from its activities. He was angry, understandably, and he took this way of showing it. Actually, of course, he was saving his enemies money; but he supposed, with his confidence, that he was depriving them of a great privilege. He had his capital now, and the devil with them.

They responded by petitioning for letters-patent permitting them to equip and send out an expedition exactly similar to that planned by Sir Humphrey. It was to be led by Mr. Carlyle, a son-in-law of Sir Francis Walsingham. Carlyle had been interested in navigation generally for some time, and he had been specifically interested in the rejected plan to settle south of the equator. Probably the Muscovy Company men supposed that when they selected him as leader they would be taking from Sir Humphrey the powerful support of Walsingham. But Walsingham continued faithful to Sir Humphrey; and Carlyle himself apparently did little or nothing to advance his proposed leadership; and eventually—presumably on the ground that Humphrey Gilbert had the prior claim—the petition was turned down. For once, the pioneer had triumphed.

There remained the Queen. Always, when everything else had been said and done, there remained the Queen. That unpredictable female invariably had the last word. And at the moment she was doubtful. She did not think Sir Humphrey ought to go.

To be sure, he could send the fleet without him, acting under his orders, responsible to him—as, not so many years later, Walter Raleigh was to do several times when the colonization zeal burnt strong within him and an aging, kittenish monarch insisted that he remain at home to amuse her. But permitting those ships to go without him—staying on land to wave them off—that was, for Sir Humphrey, unthinkable. It is quite true, he had been an armchair sailor, but only from necessity; and now, when his one big chance had come at last and everything was ready, he could not tolerate the thought of not going with his own men.

It was all very well for brother Walter to remain. Walter was definitely a favourite of the Queen; he was a young and handsome and ambitious man, at the beginning of what promised to be a career of stunning brilliancy; he was needed at Court, where his charm and wit would help so much to carry him ahead. But Sir Humphrey was in his middle forties; he was approaching the climax of his career; he had been working for this expedition before his half-brother had even attained his teens, and he had sunk all his fortune into it, his wife's fortune, too, and all the skill and loving labour at his command; it was, in every sense, *his* expedition, and quite naturally he wished to command it in person.

As for the dangers, nobody was better aware of them. For all his confidence, he knew perfectly what horrible chances he would take by putting to sea in those tiny ships. And of course it was flattering that Queen Elizabeth should take such a genuine personal interest in his welfare, and should be so honestly concerned about keeping him from peril. It was very gracious of Elizabeth.

Still, when had he ever asked or desired to be spared the hardships and dangers of this trip? The lad of twenty had laughed at death repeatedly. Did they suppose that the man of forty-three, just because he happened to be of a modest and scholarly disposition, was going to find himself possessed of less courage? As a

THE GREAT ADVENTURE BEGINS 161

captain, a colonel, even as a general, he had never asked the men under him to do anything he was not willing to do himself. He had always been, literally as well as figuratively, a leader in the field. And why shouldn't he continue in that attitude, now that he was turning to the sea?

But Elizabeth hesitated, pursed her lips, shook her head. Sir Humphrey went ahead with his preparations, superintending these on the scene, in person; while Walter Raleigh capably represented the Great Dream at Court.

There were to be five ships, and this time there was to be no troublesome Knollys. So large a fleet as the first one was not necessary, since fighting was to be avoided if possible. There was much less fuss about the preparations for this voyage. Sir Humphrey still was a poor gamble in the eyes of most Englishmen, and his second enterprise did not excite so much attention as his first; it did not partake of the nature of a public event; there was nothing official, or even semi-official, about it.

The Queen had contributed no ships. Brother Walter had contributed one, the *Bark Raleigh*, 200 tons, something new in sailing-vessels, which he had designed himself, shipbuilding being one of his many talents.[1] This was to be the vice-admiral. The admiral, or flagship, was to be the *Delight*, 120 tons. The *Golden Hind*, 40 tons, Edward Haies of Liverpool owner and captain, was to

---

[1] It should not be confused with the *Ark Raleigh*, a much more celebrated vessel which was likewise designed by Humphrey Gilbert's gifted half-brother. The *Bark Raleigh* antedated the *Ark Raleigh* by several years, and was, as its name indicates, a smaller ship. The *Bark Raleigh* was of 200 tons burden. The *Ark Raleigh*, 92 x 33 x 15 feet, rated at 800 tons, later was renamed the *Ark Royal*, and it was Lord High Admiral Howard's flagship in the fight against the Spanish Armada. Howard disliked Walter Raleigh personally—all the Howards disliked him—but he had great respect for his ability as a ship-designer. He called the *Ark Royal* the best ship he had ever commanded, and declared he would not sail in any other.

162 THE GREAT ADVENTURE BEGINS

be the rear-admiral.[2] Then there were to be two small vessels, the *Swallow*, 40 tons, and the *Squirrel*, 8 tons.

Two hundred and sixty men were to go in these five vessels, a large portion of them in the vice-admiral, Brother Walter's ship, the pride of the fleet.

Sir Humphrey had made his usual careful preparations. Nothing was overlooked; everything, apparently, had been anticipated. Months before, he had written the sailing instructions for all ships' masters, those which were to be used off the English and Irish coasts being sealed with yellow wax, those for use after Ireland had been dropped astern being sealed with red wax—all carefully guarded against possible spies. A sufficient, if somewhat awkward, semaphore system was devised by the leader himself—signal flags in the daytime, lights at night. A code of conduct for members of the crews had been written and distributed. Several places of rendezvous had been decided upon, in case the ships were separated in storm or fog. These were in England, in Ireland, and in the New World itself. Provisions had been ordered and stowed away. Also, "for the solace of our people, and allurement of the Savages, we were provided with Music in good variety: not omitting the least toys, as Morris dancers, Hobby horses, and Maylike conceits to delight the Savage people, whom we intended to win by all fair means possible. And to that end we were indifferently furnished of all petty haberdashery wares to barter with those simple people." Captain Haies, who is quoted above, had agreed to act as historian of the enterprise. There was even an official poet—Stephen Parmenius, a friend of

[2] This was not, of course, Francis Drake's renowned *Golden Hind*. *She* was in dock at Deptford, where for almost one hundred years she was a public display and was examined by thousands of properly awed sightseers. Captain Haies' vessel, however, was named after this famous craft. It was, naturally, a popular name for English vessels at the time.

THE GREAT ADVENTURE BEGINS 163

Hakluyt's, who had burst into three hundred elegant Latin hexameters as an "Embarkation Ode," and had become so intoxicated with his own subject that he begged to be taken along; the plea was granted, and Parmenius represented Hakluyt, who was desolate at not being able to go himself.

So it all depended upon the Queen. The winter of 1582-83 passed, and spring came. Within a few months, five years of the six-year term allowed by the letters-patent for colonization would have expired, and the whole scheme might fall through. Sir Humphrey must have been wild with anxiety as he made the final arrangements; but, wisely, he permitted brother Walter to speak for him at Court. The Court was at Richmond then.

Now brother Walter, be it repeated, was an extremely presentable and accomplished courtier and poet; and in addition, he was persistent, he was eloquent, and he had the interests of this enterprise very close to his heart. He gave Elizabeth no rest. He bowed impeccably before her, he dedicated exquisite verses to her, praising her beauty, her dignity, her erudition, her unprecedented graciousness and charm. And at last he was able to send brother Humphrey this letter, with the mentioned enclosure:

"To my brother, Sir Humphrey Gilbert, Knight.
"Brother,

"I have sent you a token from her Majesty, an anchor guided by a lady, as you see; and farther, her Highness willed me to send you word that she wished you as great good-hap and safety to your ship, as if her self were there in person; desiring you to have care for your self, as of that which she tendereth; and therefore, for her sake, you must provide for it accordingly.

"Farther, she commandeth that you leave your picture with me. For the rest, I leave till our meeting, or to the report of this bearer, who would needs be the messenger of this good news. So I commit you to the will and protection of God, who send us such life or death, as he shall please, or hath appointed.

"Richmond, this Friday morning
"Your true brother,
"W. RALEGH."

The last obstacle had been surmounted. There were minor causes for delay, but the big thing, the all-important thing, had been accomplished, and the expedition was virtually ready to sail.

First there was a long conference about the route. The summer had started: it was late for embarking upon a voyage across the northern Atlantic. Some of the captains proposed going south, perhaps to the present Florida, and then feeling north along the coast; it was a plan later adopted by Walter Raleigh when he had seized the torch from the falling Sir Humphrey Gilbert and was carrying Sir Humphrey's dream through another generation and toward fulfilment. But this would be a much longer trip; it would involve getting dangerously close to the suspicious, menacing Spaniards; and besides, provisions already were low, because of the delays. It was finally agreed to sail north, direct for Newfoundland. It would certainly be possible there to reprovision the ships—there would be fishing-vessels in those parts at this time of the year.

And so, "Orders thus determined, and promises mutually given to be observed, every man withdrew himself unto his charge, the anchors being already weighed, and our ships under sail, having a soft gale of wind, we began our voyage upon Tuesday the eleventh day of June, in the year of our Lord 1583," from Causet Bay, near Plymouth.

CHAPTER XXII

OVER THE BOUNDING MAIN

THE captains of the various vessels, and the masters,[1] in conference with Humphrey Gilbert before the sailing, had agreed to make direct for Cape Race, where they were certain of finding some fishing-vessels which could help them to reprovision.

Wrote Captain Haies:[2] "Not staying long upon that Newland [Newfoundland] coast, we might proceed Southward, and follow still the Sun, until we arrived at places more temperate to our content.

"Otherwise, we doubted that sudden approach of Winter, bringing with it continual fog, and thick mist, tempest and rage of weather; also contrariety of currents descending from the cape of Florida unto cape Breton and cape Race, would fall out to be great and irresistible impediments unto our further proceeding for that year, and compel us to Winter in those North and cold regions."

[1] There was a captain *and* a master for each sizable ship in those days, the captain being the owner, or a gentleman representing the owner, while the master was the practical sailor, navigator, and active head of the crew. On smaller vessels, sometimes, the captain was his own master.

[2] Captain Edward Haies of the *Golden Hind*, mentioned in the previous chapter, is our chief authority for all details of this second Humphrey Gilbert expedition. He is an uncommonly good authority, a conscientious, upright man, very careful, observant, who liked Gilbert and sympathized with him, but who was no hero-worshipper blinded by imaginary virtues. Except where otherwise specifically noted in these three remaining chapters, passages enclosed in quotation marks are from Captain Haies' own narrative of the trip, which he wrote, soon after his return, at the request of Richard Hakluyt, who published it.

It is evident, then, that Humphrey Gilbert did not intend to colonize in Labrador or Newfoundland, as is so commonly stated in general histories, but meant rather to locate along some portion of the Atlantic seaboard nearer to the places where eventually the English *did* plant permanent colonies.

He was not going to start building houses at the first place he saw; he was going to pick the site carefully. From Newfoundland, "after our refreshing and reparation of wants, we intended without delay, by God's permission, to proceed into the South, not omitting any river or bay which in all that large tract of land appeared to our view worthy of search."

The masters were instructed to head "West southwest if the wind serve" to about the forty-third or forty-fourth degree of latitude, "because the Ocean is subject to Southerly winds in June and July," whereas this trip in March, April, or May, when the prevailing winds are westerly, had been made, Haies reports, in as little as twenty-two days.

For all their studying, their ideas of the geography of the New World were hopelessly muddled, and the maps with which they worked resemble, today, mere childish scrawls; but they did have correct information about the prevailing winds.

They were "to take a traverse from 45 to 47 degrees of latitude if we be enforced by contrary winds: and not to go to the Northward of the height of 47 degrees of Septentrional latitude by no means; if God shall not enforce the contrary: but to do your endeavour to keep in the height of 46 degrees, so near as you can possibly, because cape Race lieth about that height."

This information is from notes appended to the list of rules given to each captain and master by Humphrey Gilbert himself. That list, because it shows what careful study he had given to the subject, is worth a full reading:

"First, the Admiral [the flagship] to carry his flag by day, and his light by night.

"2 Item, if the Admiral shall shorten his sail by night, then to show two lights until he be answered again by every ship showing one light for a short time.

"3 Item, if the Admiral after his shortening of sail, as aforesaid, shall make more sail again: then he to show three lights one above another.

"4 Item, if the Admiral shall happen to hull in the night, then to make a wavering light over his other light, wavering the light upon a pole.

"5 Item, if the fleet should happen to be scattered, [by] weather or other mishap, then so soon as one shall decry another to hoist both top sails twice, if the weather will serve, and to strike them twice again: but if the weather serve not, then to hoist the main top sail twice, and forthwith to strike it twice again.

"6 Item, if it shall happen a great fog to fall, then presently every ship to bear up with the admiral, if there be wind: but if it be a calm, then every ship to hull, and so to lie at hull till it be clear. And if the fog do continue long, then the Admiral to shoot off two pieces every evening, and every ship to answer it with one shot: and every man bearing to the ship that is to leeward so near as he may.

"7 Item, every master to give charge unto the watch to look out well, for laying aboard one of another in the night, and in fogs.

"8 Item, every evening every ship to hail the admiral, and so to fall after him sailing through the Ocean: and being on the coast, every ship to hail him both morning and evening.

"9 Item, if any ship be in danger any way, by leak or otherwise, then she to shoot off a piece, and presently to hang out one light, whereupon every man to bear towards her, answering her with one light for a short time, and so to put it out again: thereby to give knowledge that they have seen her token.

"10 Item, whensoever the Admiral shall hang out her ensign in the main shrouds, then every man to come aboard her, as a token of council.[3]

"11 Item, if there happen any storm or contrary wind to the fleet after the discovery, whereby they are separated: then every ship to repair unto their last good port, there to meet again."

It will be observed that Sir Humphrey was particularly concerned with the possibility that the ships would become separated in the darkness or fog. That frequently happened to fleets in those times, even in regions where fogs were not nearly so thick or winds so treacherous, as on the north Atlantic. There are various reasons to account for this—the difficulty of handling the old ships; the general ignorance of navigation; the lack of discipline and the usual conviction of each ship's captain that *he* was correct and the admiral was wrong; the absence of fog horns, and the almost incredible fact that ships in those times were not lighted at night, even when they were travelling in fleets. Sir Humphrey's instruction to the ship masters to admonish their night watches to keep a careful lookout against ramming other ships, was not at all exceptional; such instructions, in fact, were the rule then and for some time afterward. Collisions at night, when two or more ships were keeping company, were not infrequent. This is one reason why vessels so often lost other vessels in the fleet, even in clear weather: as evening began to fall, their masters

---

[3] That is, of course, every captain and master. This list of instructions was for their benefit only, not for that of every member of the crews.

took the precaution to get far from all other ships, in order to lessen the danger of collision.

The notes Sir Humphrey has added to this list of instructions direct that if the vessels are dispersed and driven back off the coast of England, they are to rendezvous at the Scilly Isles; if the same thing happen off the coast of Ireland, they are to make for Bear Haven or Baltimore Haven. If they are not united when Cape Race is reached, then they should proceed to Cape Breton or the nearest harbor west of Cape Breton; and if that is not thought safe, "by means of other shipping," they should go to the *next* port to the west, "every ship leaving their marks behind them for the more certainty of the after comers to know where to find them." These "marks" were provided, under seal, to be opened only in an emergency. Sir Humphrey was taking no chances with possible Spanish spies; and if today his precautions seem a trifle unwieldy, they were reasonable enough then, in view of his previous experiences.

They had good weather all the first day, but a "great storm of thunder and wind" blew up that night. They fought it through, however; it was nothing but a tiny taste, a wee sample of what was yet to come.

On Thursday night—that is, the third night out—the *Bark Raleigh*, saluting the flagship as required by the instructions, additionally signalled that her captain and many members of her crew were ill. About midnight that night, and without any further signals, the *Bark Raleigh*, "notwithstanding we had the wind East, fair and good," deliberately turned about and sailed back for England.

It was a terrible loss for the fleet. Captain Haies, unable to understand it, was philosophical. "I leave it unto God," he wrote. But Humphrey Gilbert was furious. Walter Raleigh had spent £2,000 on that ship, and she was the best in the fleet, and the best equipped and provisioned. It was an outrage! At his first opportunity he wrote a letter to Sir George Peckham, begging him "to solicit my brother Raleigh to make them an example to all knaves."

There was a considerable minor scandal about the desertion of the *Bark Raleigh*. Her captain, one M. Butler, and master, Robert Davis of Bristol, explained, when they returned to Plymouth, that a pestilence had stricken the ship's crew; to have gone on, they said, would be suicide. There was an investigation, and apparently an acquittal—at least, there is no record of anybody having been punished. Walter Raleigh lost a lot of money on it; and yet so bitter were the man's enemies that some of them accused him of fitting out the ship and giving her master secret orders to desert, solely for the purpose of leaving his half-brother in the lurch. He was jealous of Sir Humphrey, they said—though they didn't say it to his face.

The *Bark Raleigh* had been the vice-admiral of the fleet, and now the *Golden Hind* assumed this position, Captain Haies being careful to record the fact that he caused his flag to be moved from the mizzen to the foretop.

Then for thirteen days—from June 15th to 28th—the four little vessels "never had a fair day without fog or rain, and winds bad, much to the west northwest, whereby we were driven southward unto 41 degrees." They had been far north of their fixed course, at forty-eight degrees, when the *Bark Raleigh* turned back.

Then the winds shifted to west south-west, and they were driven far up to the fifty-first parallel of latitude.

"Also we were incumbered with much fog and mists in manner palpable, in which we could not keep so well together, but were dissevered, losing the company of the Swallow and Squirrel upon the 20th day of July."

And so, in spite of all the precautions Sir Humphrey had taken, he had lost three of his five ships before getting halfway to the New World. The *Desire* and the *Golden Hind*, however, continued.

On Saturday, July 27th, they sighted an iceberg moving south. They were then at about the fiftieth parallel of latitude—much too far north, but there seemed to be nothing they could do about it.

On Tuesday, July 30th, they had their first glimpse of land. It was exactly seven weeks from the day they had sailed out of Causet Bay.

At first they could not see much of the Land of Dreams, because of rain and fog. When finally they did see it, they were none too pleased. It was all "hideous rocks and mountains, bare of trees, and void of any green herb." Probably it was some part of Labrador.

They proceeded south, the weather clearing, and passed Penguin Island, so named for the birds Cartier had found there, "a fowl . . . almost incredible, which cannot fly, their wings not able to carry their body, being very large, not much less than a goose, and exceeding fat."

Arriving off Baccalaos Island, just north of Conception Bay, they set up a cheer at the sight of the little *Swallow*, which had weathered all the storms and was waiting for them as per arrangement. Two strange ships, French barks, were near her.

The men of the *Swallow* likewise set up a cheer, and threw their hats and other articles of clothing into the air, not at all disturbed when these fell back into the sea. Now the men of the *Swallow* were not ordinarily possessed of such extensive wardrobes that they could afford thus to go throwing things into the ocean. There was something queer about it.

Closer inspection revealed that these sailors—Channel riffraff, unregenerate pirates, the scum of English seaports—were, in fact, "altered into other apparel."

Moreover, the men of the *Swallow*, only a short while before, had captured the two French barks standing by, one laden with salt, the other with wines. These men just had the habit of piracy and they couldn't be made to understand that it was taboo on this particular trip. Their captain, Maurice Browne, "himself was very honest and religious," Haies testifies, but he had no control over this poisonous, mutinous aggregation of jailbirds and cutthroats.

Admiral Gilbert released the two French barks and instituted an investigation into the new clothing. This clothing, it transpired, came from a Newfoundland fishing-ship; her nationality is not mentioned, and for that reason it may be guessed that she was English. The *Swallow* had hailed this ship, and the *Swallow's* men had begged for permission to go aboard and do some petty trading; they badly needed clothes, they said, and they were willing to pay for them; they promised to refrain from violence. But they broke their word the moment they reached the deck of the fisherman, which they "rifled of tackle, sails, cables, victuals & the men of their apparel: not sparing by torture, winding cords about their heads, to draw out else what they thought good." They moved fast, "like men skilful in such mischief"; and when they were leaving the ship, their cockboat was overturned, pitching them all into the Atlantic. Some of them were drowned, but the others were saved by the very men they had been robbing and torturing a few minutes before—"silly fools," Haies quite properly calls these men. They were put back on the *Swallow*, and sailed west again, leaving the fishermen to continue their eastward, homeward journey as best they could. "What became afterward of the poor Newlander, perhaps destitute of sails and furniture sufficient to carry them home, whither they had not less to run than 700 leagues, God alone knoweth," Haies adds.

Presumably the stripped vessel went down. At any rate, there is no record of any suit being brought against Humphrey Gilbert or any of his heirs or associates as a result of this incident; and if it weren't for Haies, the incident itself never would have been recorded.

Neither is there any record that Humphrey Gilbert, though disapproving of the behaviour of the men aboard the *Swallow*, ever did anything about punishing them. Perhaps he feared a general mutiny, and the failure of his enterprise, if he did so. Ship discipline was not nearly so strict then as it became soon afterward; and these particular sailors were a disagreeable, desperate lot, many of whom had embarked upon the adventure simply to save themselves from the worse fate of life in an English jail.

That same day, Saturday, August 3rd, they proceeded South to the harbor of St. John's, where they found the other lost member of the fleet, the tiny *Squirrel*.

The *Squirrel* was anchored outside of the harbor. Inside of the harbor were the ships of the Newfoundland fishing-fleet, thirty-six in all, French, English, Spanish, Dutch, Portuguese. The English, who controlled the situation here, had looked with suspicion upon the little *Squirrel*, and had ordered her to remain at anchor outside of the harbour. These men had set up a rude, an extraordinary government of their own, under which one English captain ruled as admiral every week, all taking turns; and they did not welcome strangers into their midst, even English strangers.

It was five ships against thirty-six—and many of the thirty-six, though supposedly harmless fishermen, were in fact well armed. But Humphrey Gilbert did not hesitate. Wasn't this his land? Didn't he have letters-patent from the Queen herself, so stating? These fishermen were invaders, poachers. To be sure, they did not yet understand this, but he would explain it to them without delay. He sent a smallboat into the harbour, notifying them who he was and informing them that he was coming. Then he had fighting screens erected on all decks, and all cannon loaded and primed, and so "we prepared to enter the harbour, any resistance to the contrary notwithstanding."

The dramatic effect of this entrance was somewhat spoiled by an exhibition of poor seamanship. The chief actor stumbled in the doorway as he strode out upon the stage.

The harbour at St. John's is entered only by The Narrows, a rockbound alleyway about half a mile long and two or three hundred yards wide. On the southern bank is a flat rock called "The Pancake," which is exposed at low tide—and it was low tide when Humphrey Gilbert started in. Somehow, the *Delight* went aground on "The Pancake," which was perfectly visible at the time. Haies calls it a "great oversight."

Yet it was perhaps a fortunate accident. For the suspicious English fishermen, whatever they may have thought of the newcomers, simply could not stand by and see fellow Englishmen on the rocks. They knew the harbour well; they had smaller, more easily manœuvred ships. And they went to the rescue of their newly arrived governor, and pulled him off.

The *Delight*, only slightly damaged, and her three companions, proceeded into the harbour then without further mishap, and anchored there.

A conference was called aboard the *Delight*, to which all English captains and masters were summoned. The situation was explained to the fishermen. Queen Elizabeth's charter was produced, and they were permitted to gaze upon it. Governor Gilbert informed them that he was not angry about the *Squirrel* episode; he was not going to be severe with them; on the contrary, he planned to be very lenient. They were to supply his ships with all manner of provisions; he would appoint commissioners to see that the levies were fair. This applied to foreign ships as well as English ships. The country would be claimed, formally, for Queen Elizabeth. Nobody would be molested.

The fishermen, Haies reports, were impressed, and hastened to render homage, as good English subjects should, to the representative of Her Majesty. On the other hand, Stephen Parmenius, in a letter to Hakluyt, remarks that the fishermen, "being not able to match us, suffer us not to be hunger-starved," the implication being that these fellows knew better than to resist a man like Sir Humphrey Gilbert.

Well, it may have been from a sense of duty, or it may have been from a sense of fear—or it may have been something of both—or, again, it may have been merely that the fishermen were bored with their long stay, herded in this harbour drying their fish before the tedious voyage home. At any rate, they made the promises Humphrey Gilbert had expected of them; and when the conference was dismissed they returned to their respective ships, where they "caused forthwith to be discharged all the great ordnance of their fleet in token of our welcome."

Bang! Bang! Yes, it was fitting that a great noise should be made about it. For Humphrey Gilbert at last had reached America.

CHAPTER XXIII

DISASTER

IT WAS a most amazing place in which Humphrey Gilbert now found himself. There has been nothing like it since, and I think there never had been anything like it before.

These men—these rough, tough, untutored fishermen from all parts of western Europe—foregathered in the harbour at the site of the present city of St. John's, Newfoundland, for several months of each year. They came to dry the fish they had caught on the Grand Banks in late spring and early summer. Crossing the ocean in March or April, they returned in July or August; and in this way they avoided the worst weather and took advantage of the best prevailing winds. Interested only in fish, and not at all bothered by the squabbles of their princes, the secret conferences, the pompous treaties and agreements, the "underhand wars," they got along very well together as long as the politicians left them alone.

True, it was a dull life, for them; but from this pleasant distance it seems highly colourful; and certainly it was unusual. For nine or ten months of the year St. John's was silent, deserted. But during the remaining months it was a scene of considerable activity. Sometimes there were as many as one hundred ships there at one time; they were very small ships.

The English appear to have been the bosses, most of the time. Possibly this was because of the original discovery of the place by John Cabot, as some historians have suggested. But it is much more likely that most of these men never had heard of John Cabot, and wouldn't have been interested if they did hear about him. A more logical explanation is that the English had, if not more ships, then bigger and better armed ships; England was nearer, and the English could get there earlier in the season; and also, because of the proximity of their native land, English fishermen-turned-pirates would be in a good position to raid these fellows if there should be a falling-out.

At any rate, the English in St. John's were the rulers of that curious group, summer after summer. The English captains agreed among themselves about precedent, possibly by the simple process of drawing straws, and each week one captain was the supreme chief the governor. They took turns. And as each new governor came into power, he was given a feast; it was thus that they made their entertainment.

It could not be called a colony, for the men lived on their ships, though they worked on the land much of the time, drying the fish. Nor could this taking-turn system be called a government; for it had no constitution and by-laws, no courts, no institutions of any kind except that of the temporary chief, it *could* have no written laws, for its citizens couldn't write!

It could only be called an understanding. And it seems to have worked out excellently well. Sometimes, perhaps, there were fights; but if there were, we would never hear of them, anyway. It may be that occasionally it was necessary to tap on the head some captain who wouldn't stay in his place, or to sink with all hands some ship which held a troublesome crew. But the Atlantic was a most obliging place for the concealment of bodies and other evidences of crime, and what was a man or two, a ship or two, or even more, out in that wilderness, thousands of miles from the nearest outpost of civilization? And if these little things *did* happen, as we may suppose, apparently they did nothing to break up the even tenor of life in the fish-founded commonwealth. At least, when Humphrey Gilbert entered the place he found everything in good order and very quiet. The floating, seasonal city had been there for almost fifty years before that time—though not until recently had it been so large—and it was to continue there for almost another half century before St. John's actually was founded as a permanent colony.

Humphrey Gilbert went ashore the second day—it was a Sunday—and was shown the "Garden." Haies remarks that this "Garden" was a matter of nature alone, untouched by any sort of art, and consisted of many roses, "wild, but odouriferous, and to sense very comfortable," and raspberries, "which do grow in every place." St. John's is mild in August, a pleasant location; and no doubt it was like that then.

The following day he set up a tent on the shore and summoned the whole motley population of the place around him. The Queen's colonization charter was read aloud to these startled men, and then it was interpreted into their various languages. Humphrey Gilbert formally announced that he was taking over this place and all lands for two hundred leagues in every direction, as authorized. The arms of England, engraved on a tablet of lead, were erected on a wooden pillar. A flag was flown, and cannon were fired. There were appropriate cheers from at least one portion of the audience, the members of which could understand the flag, even if they didn't know quite what all the rest of it was about.

Details of the government, Sir Humphrey announced, would be made public at some later date. For the present, there were to be only three laws—the first laws of the Empire, if we except the purely military occupation of Ireland.

Law No. 1 provided that religion, "in public exer-

SIR HUMPHREY TAKES NEWFOUNDLAND

cise, should be according to the Church of England." Nothing further was said about this; there was no mention of any other religion.

Law No. 2 asserted Queen Elizabeth's rights as sole suzerain of this territory, and provided that treason should be punishable by death, as in the Mother Country.

Law No. 3 declared that "if any person shall utter words sounding to the dishonour of her Majesty, he shall lose his ears, and have his ship and goods confiscate."

But the new governor was not going to be severe. He appointed commissioners to make food levies of the various ships in harbour; he appointed other men to study the surrounding countryside and report to him everything of any conceivable interest, particularly charging them to watch for evidences of any precious metals; he granted, at very small rentals, some pieces of land to fishermen—presumably all English, but we are not sure of this—who wished to be certain they had places to dry their fish every year. And then he dismissed the assemblage.

The fishermen, whatever they may have thought of all this, were generous with their food; and the newcomers soon were supplied with more than they had asked for in the way of "wines, marmalades, most fine rusks or biscuit, sweet oils, and sundry delicacies," besides getting daily deliveries of fresh salmon, lobster, trout, cod, and other fish.

Then, too, they were entertained—and it was no mean entertainment, either! These fishermen undoubtedly had been bored, and welcomed an excuse for another grand feast—for a series of feasts, in fact; for they insisted upon wining and dining the various captains and the admiral individually. Even at home, wrote Hales, "the entertainment had been delightful, but after our wants and tedious passage through the Ocean, it seemed more acceptable and of greater contentation, by how much the same was unexpected in that desolate corner of the world; where at other times of the year, wild beasts and birds have only the fruition of all those countries, which now seemed a place very populous, and much frequented."

It was here that Parmenius, the poet, wrote the letter to Richard Hakluyt, of which mention has been made.[1] It was here, too, that Sir Humphrey wrote a short but cheerful letter to Sir George Peckham, recommending, among other things, the punishment of those responsible for the turning-back of the *Bark Raleigh*. There were fishing-ships departing from the harbour every day now, for the season was drawing to a close; and certainly other letters must have been written and delivered; but these are the only ones that have survived.

Parmenius was one of those requested to report on the nature of the surrounding countryside. He was not as enthusiastic about it as Captain Haies, and he found great difficulty travelling because of the thick forests and many fallen trees, most of them pines. With some others, he recommended to Sir Humphrey that the forests be set afire: this, he pointed out, would give the explorers a chance to look around. Coming from a poet, this is a rather startling suggestion. Gilbert's reason for refusing to act upon it was likewise unusual. He was afraid that the sea water thereabouts would be rendered bitter by turpentine and resin flowing down into it from the streams after such a fire had been made. This might spoil the fishing; it had been reported to

---

[1] Stephen Parmenius was a native of Buda, which at that time was not consolidated with the neighbouring city of Peste. Buda was then in the hands of the Turks—which possibly accounts for the presence of Parmenius in England. He did not have a good command of the English language, and the letter to Hakluyt was written in Latin, which Hakluyt himself translated.

him that this very thing had once happened "in another port," and the fish had not returned for seven whole years. Neither man had the slightest scruple against despoiling the beauty of that virgin forest.

Certainly the fishing was the most lucrative feature of this place. ". . . of fish here is incredible abundance," Parmenius reported. ". . . the hook is no sooner thrown out, but it is eftsoons drawn up with some goodly fish."

But Sir Humphrey was hopeful of finding something more thrilling than cod and salmon. He was, Haies reports, "most curious in the search for metals, commanding the mineral man and refiner, especially to be diligent. The same was a Saxon born, honest and religious, named Daniel."

Daniel poked about for some time, found a few chunks of ore which seemed to promise nothing much, and then, one day, came bounding into the presence of Haies and Sir Humphrey, all excited. He showed them a piece of ore which he declared to be silver. If silver would satisfy them, he said, they need look no farther. He would stake his life on it—and he reminded them that his life meant as much to him as her crown to Elizabeth.

At the time, Haies, having met with some sort of accident, was not much interested and did not hear the details of the Saxon's report, which was rendered to Sir Humphrey alone. "My self at this instant liker to die than to live, by a mischance, could not follow this confident opinion of our refiner to my own satisfaction." But afterward, when he felt better, he asked Sir Humphrey about it, and Sir Humphrey replied: "Content yourself. I have seen enough." If it were not for the fact that he wished to satisfy his friends that he had searched this part of the New World thoroughly, and the added fact that he wished to investigate some lands to the south so that his sub-sovereignty, under the terms of the charter, would extend there, too—if it were not for these facts, Sir Humphrey told Captain Haies, he would sail back for England without delay.

Haies had asked, too, to see the samples of ore the Saxon had produced. "I have sent it aboard," said Sir Humphrey, meaning, of course, aboard the flagship, the *Delight*. "I would have no speech to be made so long as we remain within harbour," he added, "here being both Portugals, Biscayans and Frenchmen not far off, from whom must be kept any bruit or muttering of such matter. When we are at sea proof shall be made: if it be to our desire, we may return the sooner hither again."

"Whose answer," wrote the second-in-command, "I judged reasonable, and contenting me well."

Meanwhile, the ex-pirates were running true to form. There was one plot to take over the ships while the captains and the admiral were ashore in the tent, and to sail off with them on a freebooting expedition. This was discovered and foiled. Then another group of these industrious scoundrels moved to a near-by bay and there seized a fishing-vessel; they set the crew ashore and blithely sailed off—and were never heard from again. Still others took to hiding in the surrounding forests, and later they sneaked back to Europe, one by one, by means of other vessels.

Some had died, and many were ill. Sir Humphrey decided to send the *Swallow* back to England with the sick, who were of no use to him and might communicate their diseases to others. Captain Maurice Browne of the *Swallow* was transferred with all his men to the flagship, the *Delight*, and the captain of that ship, William Winter, boarded the *Swallow* with some of his men, to take her back.

One of those returning was William Andrews, captain of the *Squirrel*, who was ill. The commander himself decided to replace Andrews as captain of the *Squirrel*. His reason was that the tiny frigate could get up rivers and into bays where the two heavier ships would not be safe; and Sir Humphrey, as eager and excited as a boy, desired to supervise the exploration work personally. So he moved his quarters from the one hundred twenty-ton flagship to the eight-ton *Squirrel*, and had the cockleshell elaborately fitted out with fighting screens on the deck and many small cannon the *Swallow* no longer needed. This was done "more to give a show, than with judgment to forsee unto the safety of her and the men," according to Haies, who considered the *Squirrel* "overcharged," as she certainly was.

The *Swallow* then sailed away, and so, on Tuesday, August 20th, after seventeen days spent in the harbour, did the three remaining ships. They were all well stocked and provisioned now. They estimated their position at forty-seven degrees, forty minutes north latitude—which was good reckoning for those days, being only six miles too far north.

The following night they reached Cape Race, where they were becalmed for a short while. They spent some of this time catching codfish, and "in less than two hours drew in fish so large and in such abundance that many days after we fed upon no other provision."

But they had hopes for "other provision." When the wind came up again, they headed for Sable Island, twenty-five leagues seaward of Cape Breton. They had heard at St. John's that a Portuguese vessel had landed some cattle and swine there thirty years previous, and that these had multiplied considerably; and the thought of fresh pork and fresh roast beef was tempting to Englishmen who had been for so long on a fish diet.

The trip took them eight days—during which time they never sighted land—and it ended in disaster.

Tuesday, August 27th, "toward evening," soundings taken from the *Squirrel* showed white sand at thirty-five fathoms. If they had known then, what mariners know today about this particular part of the coast, they would have headed seaward promptly. Off Sable Island, which they were approaching, is a region of shifting sand bottom, much of it very shoal, with rocks at unexpected intervals—a treacherous place for any sort of ship in any sort of weather. It is also a region of much fog.

On Wednesday, "toward night," there was a south wind, and they headed west north-west. William Cox, of Limehouse, master of the *Golden Hind*, did not like this, Haies records. Richard Clarke, master of the *Delight*, afterward related that he didn't like it, either, and that he had objected twice, without avail, to Sir Humphrey, who insisted upon this course. But then, Clarke, when he testified to this effect, was trying to defend himself of a charge of criminal carelessness, and Sir Humphrey Gilbert wasn't there to answer him. The careful Hakluyt, who certainly interviewed all survivors, as was his invariable custom, and who, so far as we know, had no prejudices and sought only the truth for the benefit of the records, sides with Sir Humphrey and places the burden of the blame on Clarke. Haies is somewhat ambiguous: "We bare with the land all that night, Westnorthwest, contrary to the mind of master Cox: nevertheless, we followed the Admiral, deprived of power to prevent a mischief, which by no contradiction could be brought to hold other course, alleging they could not make the ship to work better, nor to lie otherways."

Haies might have meant Sir Humphrey by the word "Admiral" here, but it is not likely; for invariably, throughout his long narrative, he refers to Sir Humphrey as "the General," and to the flagship as the "Admiral"; and so we may assume that he meant the *Delight* here.

"The evening was fair and pleasant, yet not without token of storm to ensue," continues Haies, "and most part of this Wednesday night, like the Swan singeth before her death, they in the Admiral, or *Delight*, continued in sounding of Trumpets, with Drums, and Fifes: also winding of Cornets, Haught Boys. . . . Toward evening also we caught in the *Golden Hind* a very mighty Porpoise, with a harping iron, having first stricken divers of them, and brought away part of their flesh sticking upon the iron, but could recover only that one. These also passing through the Ocean, in herds, did portend storm. I omit to recite frivolous reports by them in the Frigate,[2] of strange voices, the same night, which scared some from the helm."

Thursday the wind rose, blowing south and east, "bringing withal rain and thick mist, so that we could not see a cable length before us."

Early in the morning, as soon as they started to take soundings, they learned that they were over flats and sands. The water would be shoal, then deep, then shoal again, in every three or four ship's lengths.

The *Delight*, largest of the ships, drawing fourteen feet of water, was leading. Haies says that no watch was kept on the *Delight*, but how he knew this is a mystery. At any rate, the warning came first from the two vessels in the rear. The *Delight* was ordered, by signals, to put about promptly and beat out for sea. She started to do so—and struck.

[2] By this is meant the *Squirrel*. She is frequently called a frigate in Haies' narrative. This does not mean, however, that she was in any way like the type of vessel known as a frigate in later times. In the sixteenth century, the words "frigate" and "pinnace" were applied indiscriminately to any small boats or ships, sometimes to mere tenders or lifeboats, sometimes to slightly larger vessels capable of crossing the ocean—but not recommended to anybody who feared the water.

She was hopelessly aground and going to pieces rapidly; her stern and "hinder parts" were smashed to bits by the high waves. Nor could the other two vessels do anything to help her, being obliged to hasten south "even for our lives into the wind's eye." They sounded as they went, holding their breaths. Seven fathom, five fathom, four—even a little less than four—then it began to get a little deeper—then four fathom again—then *three!*— and all the time "the sea going mightily and high."

But "at last we recovered, God be thanked, in some despair, to sea room enough."

Nobody had seen any of the crew of the *Delight* launching boats—or trying to launch them. Nobody had seen any of them jump overboard, clinging to rafts or poles. It was supposed that they were all lost, almost one hundred of them, almost two-thirds of what remained of the expedition. All that day and part of the next day, the *Golden Hind* and the *Squirrel* beat up and down, as near to the dangerous waters as they dared, but in the thick fog they saw no sign of any survivors; and finally they made off south.

Yet there were survivors. Stephen Parmenius, the poet, who, had he lived, surely would have given us another excellent account of this whole undertaking, was drowned. So was Daniel, the Saxon, together with his reasons for believing that there were silver mines in or near St. John's. So also was the captain, Maurice Browne, "a virtuous, honest and discreet Gentleman," even though he was over-lenient with members of his crew who would a-looting go.

But the master, Richard Clarke of Weymouth, and some others, escaped. It happened that the previous day a soldier had shot some sea fowl from the deck, and the sailors had asked permission to put overside a pinnace, or smallboat, and recapture these birds. The permission had been granted. The birds had been recovered, but for some reason not explained the pinnace was not taken in again: its place was on the deck of the *Delight*, but at the time of the wreck it was being hauled behind. When everything was lost—it was altogether too rough even to think of launching lifeboats—many of the sailors jumped overboard, and some of them, the stronger swimmers, managed to reach this pinnace and cut it loose from the wreck. They helped pull some of their comrades aboard. In all, sixteen men made the craft, including Master Clarke.

The pinnace, "the bigness of a Thames barge," had been built in St. John's and was to have been used for exploration up rivers and into bays too shallow even for the *Squirrel*. It weighed about one and one-half tons and contained at this time nothing but a single oar.

The sixteen men, overcrowding this craft, drifted for seven days and seven nights, most of the time through dense fog and on a high-running sea. For food they had only "the weeds that swam in the sea." Of water they had none, except when it rained. Once a soldier among them, one Edward Headly, proposed that they draw lots—four lots of four each—and the four who drew the smallest would lighten the load and increase the per capita consumption of seaweed, by the simple expedient of jumping overboard. But Master Clarke ruled against this.

Headly and another man died, on the fifth night, of hunger and thirst and exhaustion. The others managed to make the shore of Newfoundland, where, after a rest of three days and a wonderfully welcome diet of spring water and wild berries, they pushed along the shore for another five days, and at last reached a French ship, which conveyed them to Spain. Most of them eventually got back to England.

CHAPTER XXIV

THE END OF A PIONEER

IT TOOK the heart out of the men, that loss of the *Delight*. Thereafter the mutterings increased and there was much talk about turning about and going home from this fool's errand.

And the loss was material as well as moral. All the extra provisions and supplies, which could not be stored in the small *Golden Hind* or the much smaller *Squirrel*, had been in the *Delight*. Sir Humphrey's book and papers were there, and, what he valued more, the samples of ore the Saxon Daniel had given him, and a record of Daniel's report—these also had gone to the bottom.

Humphrey Gilbert was highly mysterious about that report of Daniel's, and its loss threw him into a violent rage. According to Haies, he lamented "the loss of his great ship, more that of the men, but most of all his books and notes, and what else I know not, for which he was out of measure grieved, the same doubtless being some matter of more importance than his books, which I could not draw from him: yet by circumstance I gathered the same to be ye Ore which Daniel the Saxon had brought unto him in the New found land. Whatever it was, the remembrance touched him so deep, as not able to contain himself, he beat his boy in great rage . . . because upon a fair day, when we were becalmed upon the coast of the New found land, near unto cape Race, he sent his boy aboard the Admiral, to fetch certain things: amongst which, this being chief, was yet forgotten and left behind. After which time he could never

THE END OF A PIONEER 189

conveniently send again aboard the great ship, much less he doubted her ruin so near at hand."

Haies, thinking to safeguard future explorers in those parts, had Master William Cox of the *Golden Hind*, and his mate, John Paul, both of Limehouse, set down separately their calculations of the course the ships had taken from Cape Race toward Sable Island. The result could hardly have been much help to mariners, for Cox and Paul, despite the fact that they were both rated as "expert men," differed greatly in their findings, Cox believing that the ships had proceeded 117 leagues from Cape Race, while Paul found that they had gone 121 leagues. Their directions, too, were very different. Neither attempted to locate the position of the shipwreck according to latitude and longitude.[1]

The two remaining ships beat about for some time after the wreck, hoping to catch sight of land when the fog lifted. They sounded fifty, forty-five and forty fathoms, and sometimes even a little less than forty, and the sounding-leads brought up now "oozie land" and now "broad shell with a little sand"—which made them believe they were close to some coast. They could see nothing at all, and the waves were running high. It was getting much colder, too, and the seamen's clothes were worn threadbare; what extra clothing they had possessed, together with the loot from the waylaid fisherman, had been stowed aboard the lost *Delight*. Also they were getting hungry, and provisions were low; nor did there seem to be any chance of restocking the gallery

---

[1] Mr. Gosling, Sir Humphrey's only previous biographer, had the Cox and Paul tables checked by a modern navigator who was familiar with those waters, and he learned that if either was correct it was the mate. While it is impossible, now, to locate the place where the shipwreck *was*, it is certain that it was *not* where Master Cox's calculations placed it: it could not have been there. But it could have been where Paul's calculations placed it.

at this time of the year. The treacherous sands and flats upon which the flagship had been pounded to pieces lay to the leeward, not far away; any time that the wind changed to south, and blew good and hard, the *Golden Hind* and the *Squirrel* would certainly follow the *Delight* to destruction. The fog continued thick, revealing nothing whatever. The rumour was out that they had somehow drifted into the Bay of St. Lawrence, which they had heard was always dangerous; and the men were uneasy.

Those aboard the *Squirrel* were begging Sir Humphrey, who alone seemed to be cheerful about things, to turn back for England. When he refused to listen to them, they lined the rail of the tiny craft, and, getting close enough to the *Golden Hind* to be seen from that ship, "they made signs of their distress, pointing to their mouths, and to their clothes thin and ragged." In this fashion the panic was communicated to the sailors of the *Golden Hind*, and they too began to beg their captain to turn back.

At last Sir Humphrey agreed to return. He summoned Captain Haies and Master Cox, who, according to Haies, opposed the plan; but they finally consented.

"Be content," Sir Humphrey told them. "We have seen enough. And take no care of expenses past. I will set you forth royally next Spring, if God send us safe home."

Haies, who was a shareholder in the enterprise, afterward insisted that he had wished to continue south, and expressed the opinion that Humphrey Gilbert had been too reckless in the business of spending other men's money. But if this was the case, he and Master Cox were the only ones in the two vessels who did not wish to return: the men were downright clamorous now, and threatening mutiny, on both vessels.

So on Saturday, August 31st, they turned back. And, lo! there was a portent. ". . . at which very instant, even in winding about, there passed along between us and towards the land which we now forsook a very lion to our seeming, in shape, hair and colour, not swimming after the manner of a beast by moving of his feet, but rather sliding upon the water with his whole body, excepting the legs, in sight, neither yet diving under, and again rising above the water, as the manner is, of Whales, Dolphins, Tunas, Porpoises, and all other fish: but confidently showing himself above the water without hiding: Notwithstanding, we presented ourselves in open view and gesture to amaze him, as all creatures will be commonly at a sudden gaze and sight of men. Thus he passed along turning his head to and fro, yawning and gaping wide, with ugly demonstration of long teeth, and glaring eyes, and to bid us a farewell, coming right against the *Hind*, he sent forth a horrible voice, roaring or bellowing as doth a lion."

Naturally they all assumed that this somewhat *blasé* walrus was a warning of disaster to come—all, that is, excepting Sir Humphrey, who "took it for Bonum Omen, rejoicing that he was to war against sich an enemy, if it were the devil."

For why not fight the devil too, that worthy opponent? *Quid non.* Why Not? It was his own motto.

The wind was with them, and they passed Cape Race on Monday afternoon, making in a little more than two days the trip which, going the other way, had taken them eight days and nights.

When they were past Cape Race, Sir Humphrey Gilbert had himself rowed to the *Golden Hind*. He had stepped on an exposed nail, and apparently his shoe leather was as thin as that of his men, for his foot was cut. He had come to have it bandaged by the surgeon, there being no such luxury aboard the tiny *Squirrel*, which carried a crew of only seven or eight men.[2]

The wind was good, but the seas were running high, and several times the *Squirrel* was "almost swallowed up." Captain Haies, Master Cox, and other friends begged Sir Humphrey to remain aboard the *Golden Hind*, for safety's sake; but he refused. They did agree, however, that both ships should show lights all night, in order that they might keep close to one another.

Sir Humphrey had barely regained his cockleshell when they ran into another storm, a nasty one.

However, they pulled through this. And when the weather was clear again, Sir Humphrey returned to the *Golden Hind* for another conference. There he "made merry" with "the Captain, Master and company . . . and continued there from morning until night." They talked of many things; but Haies remarks that Sir Humphrey, who previously had entertained no high opinion of "these North parts of the world," now invariably brought the conversation back to Newfoundland. He still was highly mysterious about his interest in that place. But it was noticed that after Daniel's report he had ceased giving out large grants of land in the north countries—land with which he had previously been so very generous.

He was all optimism. He told them about the expedition he would fit out the following spring—two expedi-

---

[2] It is well to emphasize how very small the *Squirrel* was, even in those days of small ships. It was one-fifteenth the size of the lost *Delight*, one-fifth the size of the surviving *Golden Hind*, itself a tiny vessel. It was surely smaller than any of the three celebrated ships with which Christopher Columbus first crossed the ocean. Frobisher's first flagship, the *Michael*, was so tiny that the Yorkshire man had been able to lean over the deck rail and grab an Eskimo seated in a kayak; yet even the *Michael* was two and a half times as heavy as the *Squirrel*. And if you like a modern contrast, the gross tonnage of the North German Lloyd liner *Bremen* is just 5,750 times as great as was that of the *Squirrel*.

tions, rather: one to go to Newfoundland, the other to explore the southern portion of this great land of his. It is significant that he promised to assign the captain and master of the *Golden Hind* to the southern voyage of discovery, "and reserved unto himself the North, affirming that this voyage had won his heart from the South, and that he was now become a Northern man altogether."

Naturally they asked him where he was going to get the capital for such an expensive undertaking—he, a bankrupt, a failure.

"Leave that to me," said Humphrey Gilbert. "I will ask a penny of no man. I will bring good tidings unto her Majesty, who will be so gracious to lend me £10,000."

Making merry "from morning until night" is conducive to optimism, to be sure; but Humphrey Gilbert, for all his past experiences, always retained his perfect faith in Queen Elizabeth; and he seems never to have questioned for an instant that his boyhood friend would lend him this staggering sum without any other security than his own word as to what one foreigner, now dead, had reported.

Yes, he was boundlessly confident. He said that he thanked God with all his heart for what he had seen, "the same being enough for us all," he added, "and we need not seek any further." This last he repeated again and again.

When it came time to go, his friends once again pressed him to remain aboard the larger, safer vessel. And once again he refused. They begged him, pleaded with him. They told him that travelling in so small a craft as the *Squirrel*, so heavily overloaded, in the north Atlantic at this time of the year, was something very close to plain, ordinary suicide.

And he answered: "I will not forsake my little company going homeward, with whom I have passed so many storms and perils."

Haies was downright angry about it. There had been whispers, before Sir Humphrey quit England, that the man was afraid of the ocean. *Afraid!* He had heard those whispers, and of course he was furious. Haies assumes that his only reason for insisting upon a return to the *Squirrel* at this juncture was his desire to prove his own courage to the world: ". . . this was rather rashness, than advised resolution, to prefer the wind of a vain report to the weight of his own life."

But I think not. Humphrey Gilbert had no need to prove that he was a brave man; and while vanity, admittedly, is a puissant inspiration, I think that in this he was displaying sheer heroism and nothing else.

"I will not forsake my little company." It was exactly like the man, exactly the sort of thing he *would* do.

So he had himself rowed back to the cockleshell. From the *Golden Hind* they supplied him with further provisions, sorely needed aboard the *Squirrel*, "and so we committed him to God's protection."

And as though God were waiting for this very thing to happen, a terrible storm burst upon them almost immediately afterward.

They had just passed the longitude of the Azores, as they calculated, and were sailing "into the height and elevation [latitude] of England." The gale was terrific, and the waves, Haies says, were high and pyramid-wise. "Men which all their life time had occupied the Sea, never saw more outrageous Seas."

Moreover, those aboard the *Golden Hind* observed on the mainyard of that vessel, one Castor and Pollox apparition—one, and only one, little dancing fire in the air. This was bad, the sailors averred. It was bad enough to see *several* of these fires, but *one*, alone, invariably spelled a wreck.

THE END OF A PIONEER

On Monday, September 9th, in the afternoon, the *Squirrel* again and again was almost swamped. The storm had not abated; if anything, it had grown worse. Those on the *Golden Hind*, themselves in terrible danger, watched the tiny *Squirrel* as the waves hurled her about: they were fascinated. They saw Sir Humphrey Gilbert "sitting abaft with a book in his hand." Whenever the two vessels got close enough, Sir Humphrey would wave cheerfully to those on the *Golden Hind*, calling out each time: "We are as near to Heaven by sea as by land!" This happened repeatedly.

The night came, and there was no let-up in the storm. Then, at about midnight, or a little after, "the Frigate being ahead of us in the *Golden Hind*, suddenly her lights were out, whereof as it were in a moment, we lost the sight, and withal our watch cried, the General was cast away, which was too true. For in a moment, the Frigate was devoured and swallowed up by the Sea."

They lingered in the vicinity all that night; and the next day, when the weather had cleared and they had started for England again, they were careful to stop every passing sail and give out news of the disappearance, with instructions for searching and with tokens for Sir Humphrey Gilbert in case the *Squirrel* somehow were sighted and saved. But of course the *Squirrel* was not.

The *Golden Hind*, badly battered, reached Falmouth on Sunday, September 22nd.

BIBLIOGRAPHY

ADDLESHAW, PERCY, *Life of Sir Philip Sidney*
ANTHONY, KATHERINE, *Queen Elizabeth*
ASCHAM, ROGER, *The Scholemaster*
BENSON, E. F., *Sir Francis Drake*
BIRCH, DR. THOMAS, *Life of Ralegh*, contained in the 1829 edition of Raleigh's *Works*
——————— *Memoirs of the Reign of Queen Elizabeth, from the Year 1581 till her Death*
BRUSHFIELD, DR. THOMAS M., *Remarks on the Ancestry of Sir Walter Ralegh*
CAMDEN, WILLIAM, *The History of the Most Renowned and Victorious Princess Elizabeth, late Queen of England*
CAMPBELL, JOHN, *Lives of the British Admirals and other Eminent British Seamen*
CASTIGLIONI, BALDESSARE, *Cortigiano*, translated as *The Courtier*, by Sir Thomas Hobey, 1561
CAYLEY, ARTHUR, *The Life of Sir Walter Raleigh, Knt.*
CHAMBERLIN, FREDERICK, *Private Character of Queen Elizabeth*
CHIDSEY, DONALD BARR, *Sir Walter Raleigh: That Damned Upstart*
CHURCHYARD, THOMAS, *Generall Rehersall of Warres*
CORBETT, ADMIRAL SIR JULIAN, *Drake*
——————— *Drake and the Tudor Navy*
CREIGHTON, BISHOP MANDELL, *Queen Elizabeth*
——————— *The Age of Elizabeth*
DARK, SIDNEY, *Queen Elizabeth*
DE SELINCOURT, HUGH, *Great Raleigh*
DICTIONARY OF NATIONAL BIOGRAPHY
EDWARDS, EDWARD, *The Life of Sir Walter Ralegh*, the second volume containing Raleigh's letters complete
FROUDE, JAMES ANTHONY, *English Seamen in the Sixteenth Century*
——————— *History of England from the Fall of Wolsey to the Death of Elizabeth*
——————— *The English in the West Indies*
FULLER, REV. THOMAS, *History of the Worthies of England* (reprint, 1811)

GILBERT, SIR HUMPHREY, *A Discourse written by Sir Humfrey Gylberte, Knight, to prove a passage by the Northwest to Cataia and East India* (the *Discourse of the Northwest Passage*)
——————— *A Discourse how Hir Maistie may annoy the Ki. of Spayne*
——————— *A Discourse hoe hir Matie may meete with and annoy the K. of Spayne*
——————— *Queen Elizabeth's Achademy*
GOSLING, WILLIAM GILBERT, *Labrador: Its Discovery, Exploration and Development*
——————— *Life of Sir Humphrey Gilbert*
GOSSE, PHILIP, *Hawkins*
HAIES, CAPTAIN EDWARD, *A Report of the Voyage and Success Thereof, Attempted in the year of our Lord 1583, by Sir Humfrey Gilbert, Knight, etc.*
HAKLUYT, RICHARD, *The Principal Navigations, Voyages, Traffiques and Discoveries of the English Nation*
HARRISON, G. B., *An Elizabethan Journal*
HARRISON, WILLIAM, *See* HOLINSHED
HOBEY, SIR THOMAS, *See* CASTIGLIONI
HOLINSHED, RICHARD, *Holinshed's Chronicles of England, Scotland, and Ireland*, second edition reprint, 1807, by Raphael Holinshed, William Harrison and others; augmented and continued from 1577 to 1586 by John Hooker, alias Vowell
HOOKER, JOHN, *See* HOLINSHED
HUME, DAVID, *History of England*
HUME, MARTIN A. S., *Philip II of Spain*
——————— *Sir Walter Raleigh: The British Dominion in the West*
——————— *The Courtships of Queen Elizabeth*
——————— *The Great Lord Burghley: A Study in Elizabethan Statecraft*
JONES, CHARLES G., *Recollections of Royalty, from the Death of William Rufus in 1100, to that of the Cardinal York*
KINGSLEY, CHARLES, *Sir Walter Ralegh and his Time*
LEE, SIR SIDNEY, *Great Englishmen of the Sixteenth Century*
LINGARD, REV. DR. JOHN, *History of England*
MARSHALL, BEATRICE, *Sir Walter Raleigh*
MCFEE, WILLIAM, *The Life of Sir Martin Frobisher*
MERRIMAN, R. B., in *American Historical Review*, XIII, p. 480
NICHOLAS, SIR HARRIS, *Memoirs of the Life and Times of Sir Christopher Hatton, K. G.*

BIBLIOGRAPHY

OBER, F. A., *Life of Sir Walter Raleigh*
OLDYS, WILLIAM, *Life of Sir Walter Ralegh, in the Works*
PARKS, GEORGE BRUNNER, *Richard Hakluyt and the English Voyages*, edited by James A. Williamson
PARMENIUS, STEPHEN, letter to Richard Hakluyt, published in *The Principal Navigations*, etc.
POLLARD, A. F., *The Political History of England*, Vol. VI, from the Accession of Edward VI to the Death of Elizabeth
PROTHERO, G. W., *Select Statutes and Other Constitutional Documents Illustrative of the Reigns of Elizabeth and James I*, third edition, 1906
PURCHAS, SAMUEL, *Purchas His Pilgrims*
RALEIGH, SIR WALTER, *The Works of Sir Walter Raleigh, Kt.*, eight volumes, 1829, containing biographies by Oldys and Birch
READ, CONYERS, *Mr. Secretary Walsingham and the Policy of Queen Elizabeth*
RODD, SIR RENNELL, *Sir Walter Raleigh*
ST. JOHN, J. A., *Life of Sir Walter Raleigh*
SELINCOURT, *See* DE SELINCOURT
SHIRLEY, JOHN, *The Life of the Valiant & Learned Sir Walter Ralegh, Kt.*
SLAFTER, REV. CARLOS, *Sir Humfrey Gylberte, and His Enterprise of Colonization in America*, a collection of papers, letters, narratives, etc., published privately by the Prince Society, and containing a Memoir by Dr. Slafter, the editor
SMITH, CHARLOTTE FELL, *John Dee*
SOUTHEY, ROBERT, *Lives of the British Admirals*
STEBBING, WILLIAM, *Life of Sir Walter Ralegh*
STOW, JOHN, *Annals*
STRICKLAND, AGNES, *The Queens of England*
TAYLOR, I. A., *Sir Walter Raleigh*
THEOBALD, MR., *Memoirs of Sir Walter Raleigh*, second edition, 1719
TYTLER, PATRICK FRASER, *Life of Sir Walter Raleigh*
VOWELL, JOHN, *See* HOLINSHED
WALDMAN, MILTON, *Sir Walter Raleigh*
WILLIAMS, SIR ROGER, *The Actions of the Lowe Countries*
WILLIAMSON, JAMES A., *Maritime Enterprise, 1485-1558*
———— *See also* PARKS
WILSON, VIOLET A., *Queen Elizabeth's Maids of Honour, and Ladies of the Privy Chamber*

INDEX

Addleshaw, Percy, 152
Ager, Anne, see Lady Gilbert
Ager, Sir Anthony, 51
Ager, William, 155
Agincourt, battle of, 59
Alba, Duke of, 75
Albertus, 90
Alexander VI, Pope, 28, 81
Alfred, King of Westsaxe, 88
Allen, Cardinal, 150
Amiens, siege of, 55
Amundsen, Roald, 87
Andrews, Captain William, 182-3
Appianus, 88
Ardenburgh, 71, 73
Aristotle, 88
Ascham, Roger, 95
Ashley, Katherine, 11

Baccalaos Island, 171
Bacon, Francis, 95, 111
Bacon, Sir Nicholas, 95
Baffin, William, 87
Bahamas, the, 118
Baltimore Haven, 169
Barbarossa, Emperor Frederick, 89
Barros, John, 89
Bear Haven, 169
Benson, E. F., 140
Bergen-op-Zoom, 76
Bermuda, 118
Blaskely, Sound of, 42
Blois, Treaty of, 16, 71
Boleyn, Anne, 11, 15
Borgia, Rodriguez, see Alexander VI
Borington, 4
Borough, Stephen, 27
Bourbons, the, 22
Bristol, 154

Brixham, 3
Browne, Captain Maurice, 172, 182, 186
Bruges, 71-3
Burghley, Lord, 37, 42, 44 (footnote), 48 (footnote), 49-51, 60-1, 74-5, 88, 95, 155
Butler, Sir Edward, 46
Butler, Captain M., 170
Butler, Thomas, see Ormond
Butlers, the, 37, 143 (footnote)
Button, Sir Thomas, 87
Bylot, Robert, 87

Cabot, John, 176-7
Cabot, Sebastian, 27, 29, 40, 89
Cabots, the, 27
Cadiz, 118
Calais, 22, 33, 51, 67
Cambridge, 28, 86, 96
Cape Breton, 27, 165, 169, 183
Cape of Good Hope, 89
Cape Race, 165, 169, 183, 188-9, 191
Carew, George, 125
Carew, George, of Okington, 125
Carew, Sir Peter, 9, 41, 45-6
Carlyle, Mr., 82, 159
Cartier, Jacques, 89, 171
Castiglione, Baldessare, 95
Cathay, Company of, 106-8
Causet Bay, 164, 171
Cecil, Sir William, see Burghley
Cham of the Tartars, 41-2
Champernoun, Sir Arthur, 9, 41-2
Champernoun, Charles, 125
Champernoun, Gawen, 26
Champernoun, Katherine, 3, 4, 5, 8
Champernoun, Sir Philip, 3

INDEX

Champernouns, the, 26
Chancellor, Richard, 27, 42
Charles V, Emperor of Austria, 7, 8, 64
Charles IX, King of France, 64, 70
Chartres, Vidame de, 29
Chaucer, Geoffrey, 86
Churchyard, Thomas, 52-3
Clarke, Richard, 184, 186-7
Collinson, Captain Richard, 87
Columbus, Christopher, 2, 26, 27, 80 (footnote), 91, 192 (footnote)
Compton, 3, 4, 55
Conception Bay, 171
Cork, 143 (footnote)
Coronado, Francisco, 89
Cortez, Hernando, 122
Courtenay, Edward, see Devonshire
Cox, William, 184, 189-90, 192
Crantor the Greek, 88
Crecy, battle of, 59
Crofts, Sir James, 9
Cunningham, William, 28

Daniel the Saxon, 181, 186, 188, 192
Dart, the, 3
Dartmouth, 130
Davis, John, 87
Davis, Robert, 170
Dee, Dr. John, 78-9, 149
De Gomara, Francisco, 89
de' Medicis, Catherine, 70
de Mendoza, Bernardino, 123-5, 128, 130, 132-6, 148, 151-2, 156
Demongenitus, Franciscus, 88
de Montgomerie, Count, 26
de Montgomerie, Gabrielle, 26
Denny, Richard, 125-6, 128
de Reux, Count, 72
Devereux, Robert, see Essex
Devonshire, Edward Courtenay, Earl of, 9
Dieppe, 22-3

Domara, 28
Don Carlos, 20
Douai, 150
Drake, Sir Francis, 81, 84, 129, 137-42, 145, 148, 162 (footnote)
Drakes, the, 26
Dublin, 50
Dudley, Ambrose, see Warwick
Dudley, John, see Warwick
Dudley, Robert, see Leicester

Eden, Richard, 28-9
Edward VI, King of England, 6-8, 20-1
Elizabeth, Queen of England: as princess, 6, 7, 9-17; becomes queen, 18-21; dealings with Huguenots, 22-3; indifference to geography, 25, 28, 30-3; attitude toward Ireland, 34, 36-8; denies Gilbert's first petition, 39-40; attitude toward Irish colonization, 41-4, 46; sends Gilbert back to Ireland, 49, 50; politics, 55-9; her parsimony, 60-1; behavior toward Low Countries, 62-3, 65, 67-70, 74-5, 77; discourages exploration, 79-84, 86; receives academy proposition, 95, 100; health, eccentricities, 101-3; grants colonization charter, 106-7, 111-4, 116, 118-9, 121-5, 129-31, 135-6; attitude toward Catholics, 150-1, 153; objects to Gilbert's second voyage, 155-7, 159-60, 163-4; Newfoundland claimed for her, 174-5, 178-9, 181, 193
Essex, Robert Devereux, second Earl of, 145
Eton, 8, 25

Falmouth, 195
Fellowship of English Merchants for the discovery of new trades, see Merchant Adventurers

INDEX

Ferdinand and Isabella, 80 (footnote)
Fernandez, Simon, 78, 125, 131, 133
Ficinus, Marsilius, 88
Fitzmaurice, James, 45, 51, 137, 144
Flushing, 67-8, 70-1, 73-5
Fortescues, the, 26
Fox, Luke, 87
Fracastorius, Hieronymus, 89
Frisius, Gemma, 88
Frobisher, Martin, 52, 78, 85-7, 103-9, 133, 192 (footnote)
Frobisher's Straits, 108
Fuggers, the, 8
Fulton, Robert, 2

Galmeton, 3
Gardiner, Bishop, 14
Gascoigne, George, 63, 86-7
Gascoigne, Sir John, 86
Gastaldus, 88
Geraldines, the, 37, 143 (footnote)
Gerrard, Sir Thomas, 149-51
Gilbert, Adrian, 3, 4, 125
Gilbert, Anthony, 55
Gilbert, Arthur, 55
Gilbert, Humphrey, junior, 55
Gilbert, Lady Humphrey, 51, 55, 128, 155
Gilbert, Sir Humphrey: background and childhood, 1-5; at Eton, 8; as page to Princess Elizabeth, 9-13, 15-6; attitude toward queen, 19; passion for geography, 21; at Havre de Grace, 22-4; studies of geography and navigation, 25-30, 32; in Ireland, 33-5, 37-8; presents first exploration petition, 39; made a colonel, 40; his Irish colonization plan, 41-2; fighting record in Ireland, 43-4; knighted, 45; fighting, 46-50; marriage, 51; meets Frobisher, 52; his brutality, 53-4; in Parliament, 55-7; made Surveyor-General, 58-9; interest in Meadley experiments, 60-1; goes to Low Countries, 62-4, 67-9; campaign in Low Countries, 70-7; plans southern exploration, 78-80, 82-4; publication of his "Discourse," 85-92; his ideas on education, 93-100; interest in Frobisher's enterprises, 101-5, 107-8; gets his colonization charter, 110-23; first voyage, 124-36; back to Ireland, 136-7; compared with Drake, 139-42; his modesty, 143-5; plans for colony, 147-8; Catholic interest in his plans, 149-52; raising funds, 153-62; starts second voyage, 163-70; sights land, 171-3; lands, 174-6; claims Newfoundland for queen, 178-83; wreck of "Delight," 184-87; Gilbert's death, 188-95
Gilbert, John, 3, 4, 21, 32-3, 51, 55, 125, 155
Gilbert, John, son of Sir Humphrey, 55
Gilbert, Otho, son of Sir Humphrey, 55
Gilbert, Sir Otho, 3, 4, 6, 21, 32
Gilbert, Otis, 3, 4
Gilbert, Raleigh, 55
Gomara, see de Gomara
Gorges, the, 26
Gosling, W. G., 189 (footnote)
Gower, John, 86
Greenway, 3, 4, 55
Greenwich, 6
Grenville, Sir Richard, 41, 82
Grenvilles, the, 26
Grey, Lady Jane, 7
Grey, Lord, of Wilton, 143
Guise, Duke of, 69
Guises, the, 22-3
Guyccardinus, 88

INDEX

Haies, Captain Edward, 134, 161-2, 165-6, 169-70, 172-5, 178-86, 188-95
Hakluyt, Richard, junior, 27, 78, 128, 132, 154, 158, 163, 165, 175, 180
Hall, Captain C. F., 109 (footnote)
Hall, James, 87
Hampton Court, 16
Hansford, 3, 4
Hatfield, 16
Hatton, Sir Christopher, 155
Havre de Grace, 22-4, 26, 29, 67, 83, 98-9
Hawkins, John, 81
Hawkins, William, 27, 125
Hawkridge, William, 87
Headly, Edward, 187
Henry VII, King of England, 80 (footnote)
Henry VIII, King of England, 6, 11, 14, 15, 20, 103
Hobey, Sir Thomas, 95
Hooker, John, 25, 133-4
Horsey, Sir Edward, 125
Howard, Lord High Admiral, 161 (footnote)
Hudson, Hendrick, 87
Hudson's Straits, 108
Huguenots, the, 22-3, 26, 29, 67, 69, 70, 75, 101, 124, 152-3
Humber, the, 6
Hunter, 88

Isle of Wight, 131

James, Thomas, 87
Jenkinson, Anthony, 27, 42, 78-9, 89-91

Kenilworth, 86
Kilkenny, 44
Kilmallock, 44
Knight, John, 87
Knockfergus, 44
Knollys, Henry, 125-6, 128, 130-1

Leicester, Robert Dudley, Earl of, 42, 60-1, 65, 86, 145, 155
Lime Host, see Limehouse
Limehouse, 55, 184, 189
Lime Hurst, see Limehouse
Limerick, 44 (footnote), 48 (footnote)
Lincoln, Lord High Admiral, 80
Lock, Michael, 105, 109
Locke, John, 27
London Tower, 12, 14, 16, 56, 106, 109
Lough Foyle, battle of, 38-9

Maffaei, 28
Magellan, Fernando, 29, 140
Magellan's Straits, 89, 138 (footnote), 140
Martyr, Peter, 28, 88
Mary, Queen of England, 6-8, 12-21, 23, 67, 79
McClure, Sir Robert, 87
McFee, William, 104 (footnote)
Meadley, William, 60-1, 97 (footnote)
Medicis, see de' Medicis
Mela, 26
Mendoza, see de Mendoza
Menendez, Pero, 152-3
Mercator, 28, 78
Merchant Adventurers, the, 29, 30, 39, 40, 79, 85, 87, 90, 101, 154, 158-9
Mermaid Tavern, 86
Merriman, R. B., 151 (footnote)
Michiele, 11
Middleburgh, 73-4
Mondragon, General, 76
Montgomerie, see de Montgomerie
Morgan, Captain Miles, 126, 131-2, 134
Morgan, Thomas, 67-8, 72 (footnote), 73, 76
Mortlake, 78
Mountjoy, Lady, 61
Muenster, Sebastian, 28, 88

INDEX

Muscovy Company, the, see Merchant Adventurers

Nassau, Count Louis of, 64-5
Nepos, Cornelius, 89
New Haven, see Havre de Grace
Nowel, M., 88
Nunnius, Aluarus, 89

Ochther the Saxon, 88
Offewell, 4
O'Neil, Shan, 35-6, 38
Orange, Prince of, 64-5, 76, 99, 115
Ormond, Thomas Butler, Earl of, 143 (footnote), 144
Ortelius, Abraham, 78, 88
Otterden, 51
Oviedo, 28
Oxenham, John, 138 (footnote)
Oxford, 8, 25, 96

Pachedo, Pedro, 73
Parmenius, Stephen, 162-3, 175, 180-1, 186
Paul, John, 189
Peckham, Sir George, 82, 125, 149-51, 155, 170, 180
Penguin Island, 171
Penkewell, Philip, 4
Perreira, 28
Philip II, King of Spain, 7, 8, 12-3, 15-8, 20-1, 64, 77, 115-8, 124, 130, 132, 135, 137, 139, 148, 151-4
Philo the Jew, 88
Pickman, 74
Pigabetta, 29
Pimsoll's Mark, 137
Pius V, Pope, 150
Pizarro, Francisco, 122
Plague, the, 24, 98-9
Plato, 88
Pliny, 26, 89
Plymouth, 55-6, 80, 118, 126, 131, 164, 170
Pollard, A. F., 13

Pope's Line, the, 28, 81
Portland Castle, 106, 109
Proclus, 88
Ptolemy, 26
Puteanus, Bernard, 88
Pyckman, see Pickman

Radcliffe, Thomas, see Sussex
Raleigh, Carew, 125, 131
Raleigh, George, 3
Raleigh, Katherine, 3
Raleigh, Walter, senior, 4, 8, 9
Raleigh, Sir Walter: friend and half brother of Humphrey Gilbert, 2, 4, 5, 87, 101-2, 111, 125, 131, 133; in Ireland, 142-5; rise in court, 146-7; assists Humphrey Gilbert, 153, 159-64; his ship turns back, 169-70
Raleighs, the, 26
Randolph, Colonel Edward, 38-9
Reformation, the, 13
Reniger, Robert, 27
Resolution Island, 107
Reux, see de Reux
Ribault, Jean, 29, 152-3
Richmond, 163
Ross, 42
Rouen, 22-3

Sable Island, 189
St. Bartholomew's Massacres, 76
St. John's, Newfoundland, 173-4, 176-8, 186-7
St. Lawrence, Bay of, 190
St. Lawrence Island, 115-6
St. Leger, Warham, 41
Sandridge, 3
Sara, see t'Zaareets
Savoy, Emmanuel Philibert, Prince of, 20
Schetz, the, 8
Scilly Isles, the, 169
Scott, Sir Walter, 86
Severn, the, 6

INDEX

Seville, 118
Seymour, Edward, see Somerset
Siculus, Marinæus, 88
Sidney, Sir Henry, 37-8, 40, 42, 44-5, 50, 85, 155
Sidney, Sir Philip, 38, 149, 152
Sluys, 71
Smerwick, 142
Smyth, Sir Thomas, 60-1
Somerset, Edward Seymour, Duke of, 6
Souburg, 73
Southampton, 154-5
Strabo, 26, 88
Stukeley, Thomas "Lusty," 83
Sussex, Thomas Radcliffe, third Earl of, 37, 38, 155

Tergoes, 73, 76
Thevitt, Anthony, 29
Tomson, Robert, 22
Torbay, 3
Towerson, William, 27
Tramasinus, Michael, 88
Tramontanus, 88
t'Zaareets, General, 71, 72 (footnote), 73, 76

Vancouver, B. C., 140
Vauasor, Andreas, 88

Venetus, Paulus, 89
Villegagnon, Nicolas, 29

Walfled Bay, 136
Walsingham, Sir Francis, 42, 61, 64-6, 82, 126, 143, 148, 151-3, 155-7, 159
Ward, Armagil, 27
Ward, Captain John, 44 (footnote), 49
Warwick, Ambrose Dudley, Earl of, 23, 24, 85, 155
Warwick, John Dudley, Earl of, 6
Waymouth, George, 87
Wentworth, Peter, 56
William the Conqueror, 2, 3
Williams, Sir Roger, 72 (footnote), 73
Willoughby, Sir Hugh, 27, 42, 79, 91
Winter, Captain William, 182
Winter, Sir William, 109
Woodstock, 12, 16
Wright Brothers, 2
Wyatt, Sir Hugh, 9, 12, 15
Wyatt's Rebellion, 9, 12, 15

Zaareets, see t'Zaareets
Zara, see t'Zaareets
Zieglerus, Jacobus, 90